MAX-PLANCK-GESELLSCHAFT

Universität Augsburg University

TECHNISCHE UNIVERSITÄT MÜNCHEN

THE GEORGE WASHINGTON UNIVERSITY

WASHINGTON, DC

MIPLC Studies

Volume 38

Stephanie Elfering

Unlocking the Right to Data Portability

An Analysis of the Interface with the Sui Generis Database Right

Nomos

MIPLC Munich Intellectual Property Law Center
Augsburg München Washington DC

This publication was supported by the Max Planck Society.

The **Deutsche Nationalbibliothek** lists this publication in the Deutsche Nationalbibliografie; detailed bibliographic data are available on the Internet at http://dnb.d-nb.de

a.t.: Munich, Master Thesis Munich Intellectual Property Law Center, 2018

ISBN 978-3-8487-6148-7 (Print)
978-3-7489-0270-6 (ePDF)

British Library Cataloguing-in-Publication Data
A catalogue record for this book is available from the British Library.

ISBN 978-3-8487-6148-7 (Print)
978-3-7489-0270-6 (ePDF)

Library of Congress Cataloging-in-Publication Data
Elfering, Stephanie
Unlocking the Right to Data Portability
An Analysis of the Interface with the Sui Generis Database Right
Stephanie Elfering
76 pp.
Includes bibliographic references.

ISBN 978-3-8487-6148-7 (Print)
978-3-7489-0270-6 (ePDF)

DOI: https://doi.org/10.5771/9783748902706

Published by Nomos Verlagsgesellschaft, Baden-Baden, Germany 2019.
Printed and bound in Germany.

1st Edition 2019

Table of Contents

Abstract

The European Union (EU) data economy could reach EUR 739 billion in value by 2020 if policy and legal framework conditions are put in place in time. The first step towards the enhancement of the internal market dimension of data has already been taken by the EU in 2016 with the adoption of the General Data Protection Regulation (GDPR), which introduced the novel right to data portability (RtDP). While the RtDP's primary objective is to provide data subjects with greater control over their personal data, it also has a pro-competitive character, as a tool to decrease consumer lock-in.

The RtDP is, however, not an absolute right, as Article 20(4) GDPR sets forth that it 'shall not adversely affect the rights and freedoms of others'. This wording arguably also encompasses intellectual property rights (IPRs), which could represent a claim for controllers to not comply (or only partially comply) with a portability request. The most relevant IPR candidate in this regard is the sui generis database right (SGDR) under the Database Directive (DbD), considering that a database is commonly realised as a collection of data. Unfortunately, the Commission's recent second ex-post evaluation on the DbD did not approach such potential conflict.

Against this background, this research aims to explore and redefine the interface between the RtDP and the SGDR, taking particular account of the data economy's context. It is organized in three key parts: Part II focuses on the legal framework of the RtDP. Subsequently, Part III outlines the intersection between personal data and the SGDR. After delineating the SGDR, each element is then confronted with a personal data and RtDP scenario to determine if there is indeed a potential clash. Finally, Part IV discusses the potential issues arising from such intersection, as well as possible ways forward to solve it. This final analysis argues for a coordinated approach, which takes the big picture of the data economy into account, to provide for an effective outcome.

Keywords: GDPR, Right to Data Portability, Article 20(4), Database Directive, Sui Generis Database Right, Data Economy, Data Access Right

Acronyms and Abbreviations

B2B	Business-to-business
B2C	Business-to-consumer
BGH	*Bundesgerichtshof* (German Federal Supreme Court)
CJEU	Court of Justice of the European Union
DbD	Database Directive
DPD	Data Protection Directive
ECHR	European Convention on Human Rights
EDPB	European Data Protection Board
EDPS	European Data Protection Supervisor
EEA	European Economic Area
EU	European Union
FRAND	Fair, Reasonable and Non-Discriminatory
GDPR	General Data Protection Regulation
IoT	Internet of Things
IPR	Intellectual Property Right
ISP	Internet Service Provider
OECD	Organisation for Economic Co-operation and Development
RtDP	Right to Data Portability
SGDR	Sui Generis Database Right
SME	Small and Medium Enterprises
TFEU	Treaty on the Functioning of the European Union
WP29	Article 29 Data Protection Working Party

I. Introduction

The European Union (EU) data economy could reach EUR 739 billion in value by 2020[1] 'if policy and legal framework conditions (…) are put in place in time',[2] doubling within the next two years.[3] It is, therefore, not surprising that 'data' has become a trending buzzword and is being referenced by many as the 'new oil' of the modern data economy.[4]

The first step towards the enhancement of the internal market dimension of data has already been taken by the EU in 2016 with the reform of its data protection framework, including adoption of the General Data Protection Regulation (GDPR) regarding the processing of personal data and its free movement.[5] Among the innovations introduced to adapt the EU legal landscape to the data economy is the novel right to data portability (RtDP) laid out in Article 20 GDPR.

As a right established within a data protection legislation, the RtDP's first and main objective is to grant individual's greater control over their personal data. However, with the increase of data-based businesses (such as big data, cloud and Internet of Things (IoT)), data has acquired an economic dimension, representing a strategic element in competition between digital products and services, in view of its ability to create consumer lock-in and hinder market.[6]

1 IDC, 'European Data Market – Final Report' [2017] SMART 2013/0063, 126.

2 Commission, 'Building a European Data Economy' (Communication) COM(2017) 9 final, 2.

3 Commission, 'Towards a Common European Data Space' (Communication) COM(2018) 232 final, 1.

4 Notwithstanding the criticism of economist on such comparison, since data is not a scarce commodity and has a nonrival character.

5 Regulation (EU) 2016/679 of the European Parliament and of the Council of 27 April 2016 on the protection of natural persons with regard to the processing of personal data and on the free movement of such data, and repealing Directive 95/46/EC [2016] OJ 2 119/1 (General Data Protection Regulation – GDPR).

6 Inge Graef, *Data as Essential Facility: Competition and Innovation on Online Platforms* (Doctoral Thesis, KU Leuven Faculty of Law 2016) <https://lirias.kuleuven.be/bitstream/123456789/539854/1/Final+draft+PhD+-+Inge+Graef+-+Data+as+Essential+Facility+-+30+May+2016.pdf> accessed 15 March 2018, 146; Inge Graef, Jeroen Verschakelen and Peggy Valcke, 'Putting the Right to Data Portability into a Competition Law Perspective' (2013) <https://ssrn.com/abstract=2416537> accessed

Although the GDPR became applicable on 25 May 2018, numerous questions remain open on the extent of its scope, as well as its implementation, applicability, and enforceability. Among the questions is what Graef, Husovec and Purtova identify as the 'Silent Conflict [of the RtDP] with IP Rights'.[7]

The RtDP is not an absolute right, as Article 20(4) GDPR sets forth that it 'shall not adversely affect the rights and freedoms of others'. In view of its broad wording, 'rights of others' arguably also encompass intellectual property rights (IPRs), which could represent a claim for controllers[8] to not comply (or only partially comply) with a portability request.

The most relevant IPR candidate in this regard is the sui generis database right (SGDR) under the Database Directive (DbD),[9] considering that a database is commonly realised as a collection of data. The SGDR's broad scope grants owners the right to prevent extraction and reutilization of all or a substantial part of the contents of the database.[10] Thus, a portability request could be perceived by the SGDR's owner as adversely affecting its right.

Modernization of the legal framework and development of a data economy have been at the core of the EU's Digital Single Market Strategy.[11] Among the initiatives to foster the data-driven economy, the Commission has launched in May 2017 a public consultation on the DbD for its second

---

28 March 2018, 2; Aysem D Vanberg and Mehmet B Ünver, 'The Right to Data Portability in the GDPR and EU Competition Law: Odd Couple or Dynamic Duo?' (2017) 8 (1) EJLT 13; Barbara van der Auwermeulen, 'How to Attribute the Right to Data Portability in Europe: A Comparative Analysis of Legislations' (2017) 33 (1) CLSR 57, 61.

7 Inge Graef, Martin Husovec and Nadezhda Purtova, 'Data Portability and Data Control: Lessons for an Emerging Concept in EU Law' (2017) DP 2017-041 Tilburg Law School Legal Studies Research Paper Series No. 22/2017 <https://ssrn.com/abstract=3071875> accessed 26 March 2018, 10.

8 Article 4(7) GDPR defines 'controller' as 'natural or legal person, public authority, agency or other body which, alone or jointly with others, determines the purposes and means of the processing of personal data'.

9 Directive 96/9/EC of the European Parliament and of the Council of 11 March 1996 on the legal protection of databases [1996] OJ L 77/20 (Database Directive – DbD).

10 DbD art 7(1).

11 Commission, 'A Digital Single Market Strategy for Europe' (Communication) COM(2015) 192 final 6, 14.

ex-post evaluation.[12] The main objective was to verify 'whether the Directive is still fit-for-purpose in (…) [the] data-driven economy' and 'identify possible needs of adjustment'.[13] Unfortunately, however, the consultation did not approach the potential conflict between the SGDR and the RtDP.

Against this background, this research aims to explore and redefine the interface between Article 20 GDPR and the SGDR, taking particular account of the data economy's context. It is organized in three key parts:

Part II focuses on the legal framework of the RtDP. Special recourse will be taken from the 'Guidelines on the Right to Data Portability'[14] issued by the Article 29 Data Protection Working Party (WP29)[15] to clarify its view on the RtDP. Also, although this research focuses on the RtDP (and, consequently, on personal data) it is instructive to note that there are other legislative proposals in the EU dealing with data portability which go beyond personal data.[16]

Part III outlines the intersection between personal data and the SGDR. Is there a real potential clash that could prevent individuals from porting their personal data? To answer such question, first the SGDR is delineated and analysed, with special consideration of the applicable case-law. Thereafter, each element is confronted with a personal data and RtDP scenario.

Finally, Part IV intends to answer the question if there is a need for a re-designed approach to enable the RtDP in the context of the data economy, by considering potential issues arising from the intersection between personal data and the SGDR, as well as possible ways out.

---

12 Commission, 'Summary Report of the Public Consultation on the Evaluation of Directive 96/9/EC on the Legal Protection of Databases' (Consultation Results, 6 October 2017) <https://ec.europa.eu/digital-single-market/en/news/summary-report-public-consultation-legal-protection-databases> accessed 7 March 2018.

13 Ibid.

14 Article 29 Data Protection Working Party, 'Guidelines on the Right to Data Portability' [2017] WP242 rev 01 (WP29 Guidelines). The WP29 Guidelines are not binding.

15 The European Data Protection Board (EDPB) has meanwhile succeeded WP29 under the GDPR. WP29's documents, including the WP29 Guidelines, were endorsed by the EDPB, 'Endorsement of GDPR WP29 guidelines by the EDPB' [2018] Endorsement 1/2018.

16 Commission, 'Proposal for a Directive of the European Parliament and of the Council on Certain Aspects Concerning Contracts for the Supply of Digital Content' COM(2015) 634 final; Commission, 'Proposal for a Regulation of the European Parliament and of the Council on a Framework for the Free Flow of Non-Personal Data in the European Union' COM(2017) 495 final.

II. The Right to Data Portability

A. *Brief Overview on the GDPR*

Already in 2010, the Commission laid down the foundations for the ambitious modernization of the EU's personal data protection framework,[17] which culminated in the GDPR's enactment. It was the result of extensive reviews, consultations and studies, concluding that legislation then in place (in particular, the Data Protection Directive (DPD)[18]) could no longer cope with the new challenges emerging from technology development and globalization.[19]

The digital age changed both the economy and society, and opened a new world of possibilities for data collection, processing, storage, sharing and analysis.[20] While individuals undoubtfully benefited from new products and services, their use came intertwined with a high price in terms of data protection. The consequence was a loss of control and trust in the online environment, which the Commission considered as one of the main obstacles for the EU's digital single market strategy.[21]

Distrust in digital products and services has a direct impact on the EU's economic development. Consumer lack of confidence can prevent adoption of new digital products and services, leading to a disincentive to innovate.[22] In view of this, the Commission acknowledged the strengthening of

---

17 Commission, 'A Comprehensive Approach on Personal Data Protection in the European Union' (Communication) COM(2010) 609 final.

18 Directive 95/46/EC of the European Parliament and of the Council of 24 October 1995 on the protection of individuals with regard to the processing of personal data and on the free movement of such data [1995] OJ L 281/31 (Data Protection Directive – DPD).

19 COM(2010) 609 final (n 17) 5.

20 Commission, 'Impact Assessment Accompanying the General Data Protection Regulation and the Directive on the Protection of Individuals with Regard to the Processing of Personal Data by Competent Authorities for the Purposes of Prevention, Investigation, Detection or Prosecution of Criminal Offences or the Execution of Criminal Penalties, and the Free Movement of such Data' (Commission Staff Working Paper) SEC(2012) 72 final 7.

21 Ibid 7, 22-5.

22 Ibid 7.

individuals' rights (in particular, control over their own data) as one of the reform's key objectives.[23]

The GDPR's material scope consists of the processing of personal data (further discussed below).[24] Its territorial scope provides for a far-reaching provision: it applies to processing conducted within the context of an establishment in the EU/European Economic Area (EEA),[25] as well as cases where the establishment is outside but the processing relates to a data subject within the EU/EEA, to whom the goods or services are being offered, or whose behaviour is being monitored.[26]

Starting with the choice of secondary law,[27] to the introduction of new rights of data subjects, the GDPR is considered by many as a truly innovative and revolutionary piece of legislation.[28] The catalogue of data subjects' rights was complemented with two new ones: (i) the right to erasure (or, as commonly known, right to be forgotten),[29] and (ii) the RtDP.[30] While the former had already been recognized by the Court of Justice of the European Union (CJEU),[31] the latter has no predecessor in the realm of EU data protection law.

But before analysing the RtDP, the concept of 'personal data' has to be discussed in detail, as it is vital to determine the RtDP's scope.

---

23 COM(2010) 609 final (n 17) 5.

24 GDPR art 2(1). Article 4(2) defines 'processing' as 'any operation or set of operations which is performed on personal data or on sets of personal data, whether or not by automated means', while Article 2(2) excludes certain types of processing from the GDPR's scope.

25 GDPR art 3(1).

26 GDPR art 3(2)(a)-(b).

27 Under the DPD, significant divergences were verified across Member States' national data protection laws. To ensure a level playing field for the data economy, the Commission opted for a regulation. COM(2010) 609 final (n 17) 3; SEC(2012) 72 final (n 20) 11.

28 Carolina Banda, *Enforcing Data Portability in the Context of EU Competition Law and the GDPR* (Master Thesis, MIPLC 2017) 61, 28; Graef, Husovec and Purtova (n 7) 2; Gabriela Zanfir, 'The right to Data Portability in the Context of the EU Data Protection Reform' (2012) 2 IDPL 149, 150.

29 GDPR art 17.

30 GDPR art 20.

31 Case C-131/12 *Google Spain* [2014] ECLI:EU:C:2014:317.

B. The Concept of 'Personal Data'

Article 4(1) GDPR defines 'personal data' as 'any information relating to an identified or identifiable natural person', the so-called 'data subject'. It further specifies that an 'identifiable natural person' is in place where she 'can be identified, directly or indirectly'. Besides obvious identifiers, such as name and ID, the definition lists 'location data, an online identifier or (...) factors specific to the physical, physiological, genetic, mental, economic, cultural or social identity' as additional examples.[32]

The CJEU adopted a quite broad interpretation of the definition, especially concerning 'identifiability'.[33] In 2011, the Court held that an IP address could be personal data from an Internet Service Provider's (ISP) perspective.[34] Later, it clarified in *Breyer* that even a dynamic IP address could constitute personal data, where the controller would have the means to obtain additional information to identify the data subject.[35]

In line with the case-law, Recital 26 GDPR provides further guidance by adopting a 'test of reasonable likelihood of identification'.[36] All means reasonably likely to be used by the controller or a third party must be considered. How costly and time consuming the means are, as well as the technology available at the time of processing, have to be considered to establish identifiability.

More recently, the CJEU ruled in *Nowak* that even written answers of a candidate's exam and the examiner's comments thereto are 'personal data'.[37] It held that

> [T]he expression 'any information' (...) reflects the aim of the EU legislature to assign a wide scope to that concept [of personal data], which is not restricted to information that is sensitive or private, but potentially encompasses all kinds of information, not only objective but also subjective.[38]

---

32 Articles 4(13)-(15) GDPR further define three special categories of personal data: (i) genetic data; (ii) biometric data; and (iii) data concerning health.

33 Although case-law is still based on the DPD, considering the similarity of the provisions, the principles carry across.

34 Case C-70/10 *Scarlet Extended* [2011] ECLI:EU:C:2011:771 para 51.

35 Case C-582/14 *Breyer* [2016] ECLI:EU:C:2016:779 paras 44-49.

36 Nadezhda Purtova, 'The Law of Everything. Broad Concept of Personal Data and Future of EU Data Protection Law' (2018) 10 (1) LIT 40, 44.

37 Case C-434/16 *Nowak* [2017] ECLI:EU:C:2017:994 para 62.

38 Ibid para 34.

Taking account of the above, 'personal data' might encompass any kind of information, even non-personal and pseudonymized data[39] that, when combined with some additional data, can identify the individual.[40] Contrarily, anonymous data, ie 'information which does not relate to an identified or identifiable natural person or to personal data rendered anonymous in such a manner that the data subject is not or no longer identifiable',[41] falls outside the scope.

This leads to a very broad and context-dependent definition.[42] The main issue is the difficulty of setting a clear borderline between personal and non-personal data, which is essential for determining the GDPR's scope. This holds especially true with current improvement and exponential use of powerful data analytics.[43] Combination of constantly growing datasets and the fast development of (re)identification technologies results in a higher likelihood of two remote pieces of information culminating in identifiability.[44]

To better understand the dimension of such broad definition, take the Commission's example – home temperature sensors.[45] In a first hint, one would probably not relate data collected by such devices to personal data. However, home temperature will be considered personal data if there is a reasonable likelihood that it could be linked to a natural person. Their sensors can collect personal and non-personal data.

---

39 Article 4(5) GDPR defines 'pseudonymisation' as 'the processing of personal data in such a manner that the personal data can no longer be attributed to a specific data subject without the use of additional information, provided that such additional information is kept separately and is subject to technical and organisational measures to ensure that the personal data are not attributed to an identified or identifiable natural person'.

40 Recital 26 GDPR states that 'personal data which have undergone pseudonymisation, which could be attributed to a natural person by the use of additional information should be considered to be information on an identifiable natural person'.

41 GDPR rec 26.

42 Purtova (n 36) 47.

43 Josef Drexl, 'Data Access and Control in the Era of Connected Devices – Study on Behalf of the European Consumer Organization BEUC' (2018) BEUC <https://www.beuc.eu/publications/beuc-x-2018-121_data_access_and_control_in_the_area_of_connected_devices.pdf> accessed 9 June 2019, 48; Graef, Husovec and Purtova (n 7) 8.

44 Drexl, 'BEUC Study' (n 43) 48; Purtova (n 36) 41-2, 47.

45 COM(2017) 9 final (n 2) 9.

Hence, it is necessary to set bias on personal data aside and keep an open mind. The world has changed with technology, as does the concept of personal data.

C. The Right to Data Portability under the GDPR

Article 20 GDPR introduces an entirely novel right – the RtDP – which is considered a major legal innovation. As a personal right, only the concerned (living) data subject has a claim under the RtDP.[46] Although it is comparable to the telecom's number portability,[47] it is concomitantly something completely different, as discussed below.

1. Legislative History and Purpose

Complementing the rights of data subjects with a portability right was within the Commission's plans from the very beginning,[48] as it reported to have received queries from several individuals complaining that they were unable to retrieve their personal data from online service providers.[49]

An individual's increasing dependence on online services and the inability to easily retrieve their personal data therefrom results in high switching cost. Time and effort to change might be so burdensome, that users decide to stay with the current provider, even if better ones are available on the market.[50] This scenario is referred to as a 'lock-in effect'.

To ensure improvement on individuals' control, withdrawal from their personal data from one application or service and transfer into another one, was considered essential. The European Data Protection Supervisor (EDPS) considered the RtDP as a strategic element, a 'gateway in the digital environment to the user control which individuals are now realizing

46 According to Veil, the claim may also be asserted by a legal representative (eg a lawyer or legal guardian). Winfried Veil, 'Artikel 20 – Recht auf Datenübertragbarkeit' in Gierschmann S and others, *Kommentar Datenschutzgrundverordnung* (Bundesanzeiger 2018) 590, 600-1.

47 SEC(2012) 72 final (n 20) 28.

48 COM(2010) 609 final (n 17) 8.

49 Ibid 7.

50 SEC(2012) 72 final (n 20) 28.

they lack'.[51] Online platforms,[52] especially social networks,[53] have always been the Commission's focus. Notwithstanding the (attempted) tailoring for online platforms, the final wording is neutral, not confining its applicability to any specific sector.

The Commission's 2012 proposal for the GDPR first introduced the RtDP as an independent right under Article 18.[54] Thereafter, the European Parliament's review included it under Article 15(2a) regarding the right to access.[55] This merger was perceived as the Parliament's way of expressing its view that the RtDP is an extension of the right to access.[56] However, after discussions in the Council, the RtDP was assigned once again an independent article in the final version.[57]

During review in the Council, several delegations expressed concerns about including the RtDP in the GDPR.[58] One of the main reasons was that the RtDP could be more a matter of competition law or consumer law, rather than of data protection. As discussed, consumer lock-in was a core issue, which can represent a market entrance barrier in detriment of consumer welfare.[59]

In view of the above, it is possible to differentiate the RtDP's purpose from its rationale. While the purpose of the RtDP is to strengthen data subjects' control and build trust in the digital environment, the underlying rationale is to avoid lock-in. It is therefore recognized, that the RtDP has

---

51 EDPS, 'EDPS Recommendations on the EU's Options for Data Protection Reform' [2015] OJ C 301/1, 5 (item 3.2).

52 The concept of 'online platform' includes search engines, social networks and e-commerce platforms. Graef, *Essential Facility* (n 6) 16.

53 COM(2010) 609 final (n 17) 7.

54 Commission, 'Proposal for a Regulation of the European Parliament and Of the Council on the protection of individuals with regard to the processing of personal data and on the free movement of such data (General Data Protection Regulation)' COM(2012) 11 final, 9, 53.

55 European Parliament, 'Report on the Proposal for a Regulation of the European Parliament and of the Council on the Protection of Individuals with Regard to the Processing of Personal Data and on the Free Movement of such Data (General Data Protection Regulation)' A7-0402/2013, amendment 111.

56 Graef, Husovec and Purtova (n 7) 4.

57 GDPR art 20.

58 Council Doc ST 10614 2014 INIT (06.06.2014) 3, fn 1.

59 Barbara Engels, 'Data Portability Among Online Platforms' (2016) 5 (2) IPR 5.

concomitantly a data protection, consumer law and competition law dimension.[60]

2. Scope of the Right to Data Portability

The scope of the RtDP vests data subjects with a two-folded right: (i) a right to receive and transfer personal data[61] (indirect portability), and (ii) a right to have it transmitted directly from one controller to another[62] (direct portability).[63]

Article 20(3) GDPR clarifies that the RtDP is without prejudice to the right to erasure. Accordingly, after completion of a portability, the data subject's personal data will be both with the first controller and the data subject and/or the second controller.[64] In this regard, the RtDP differs significantly from the telecom number portability, where the first service provider does not retain the individual's number after portability conclusion. Considering such characteristic, the RtDP could arguably be a right of 'copying' or 'sharing' one's own personal data.

The indirect portability is also two-folded – it grants data subjects a right (i) to receive their personal data, and (ii) to transmit them to another controller without hindrance from the original controller. The controller has to provide the data 'in a structured, commonly used and machine-readable format', which is not defined in the GDPR. Recital 68 adds that the format should be interoperable.

The rationale of the format requirement can be inferred from the Commission's proposal – it should allow 'for further use [of the data] by the data subject'.[65] They are minimum requirements to enable reuse of the data by the individual or another controller.[66]

---

60 Inge Graef, 'Blurring Boundaries of Consumer Welfare: How to Create Synergies between Competition, Consumer and Data Protection Law in Digital Markets' (2016) <https://ssrn.com/abstract=2881969> accessed 15 March 2018, 10.

61 GDPR art 20(1).

62 GDPR art 20(2).

63 Hans-Georg Kamann and Martin Braun, 'Art. 20 Recht auf Datenübertragbarkeit' in Ehmann E and Selmayr M (eds) *Datenschutz-Grundverordnung: DS-GVO* (2nd edn, Beck 2018) 495, 502-05; Veil (n 46) 614.

64 Veil (n 46) 614.

65 COM(2012) 11 final (n 54) art 18(1).

66 WP242 (n 14) 17.

As argued by Veil, the expression 'structured format' is probably incorrect.[67] It is not the format in which the personal data is transferred that has to be structured, but rather the data itself. This seems indeed more in line with the objective of data reuse.

Considering the RtDP's applicability across sectors, the commonly used format requirement seems the most complex one to achieve, as different standards apply to different sectors.[68] Suggestions were made regarding sector-specific standards for compliance with the provision, but this would not solve the issue when portability is requested across sectors. Thus, the preferred approach would be to understand it as requiring controllers to use a format compatible with the state-of-the-art when of the portability request.[69] This would not prevent, however, adoption of sector-specific regulations where appropriate.

With regard to the machine-readable format requirement, recourse can be taken from Directive 2013/37/EU, which defines it as 'a file format that is structured in such a way that software applications can easily identify, recognise and extract specific data from it'.[70] The provision clarifies that 'documents encoded in a file format that limits automatic processing, because the data cannot, or cannot easily, be extracted from them, should not be considered to be in a machine-readable format'. A PDF file, for instance, was not considered machine-readable by WP29.[71]

Furthermore, the data subject has the right to transmit her personal data to another controller *without hindrance* from the first controller. According to the WP29 Guidelines, a hindrance is 'any legal, technical or financial obstacles placed by data controller to refrain or slow down access, transmission or reuse by the data subject or by another data controller'.[72]

---

67 Veil (n 46) 612.

68 Peter Swire and Yianni Lagos, 'Why the Right to Data Portability Likely Reduces Consumer Welfare: Antitrust and Privacy Critique' (2013) 72 MdLRev 335, 346. Drexl, 'BEUC Study' (n 43) 109 even argues that if such commonly used formats do not exist, the data subject will have no claim under the RtDP. Applicability of such a strict interpretation seems aligned with the technical feasibility requirement for direct portability, but would probably not justify a refusal in case of indirect portability.

69 Kamann and Braun (n 63) 503.

70 Directive 2013/37/EU of the European Parliament and of the Council of 26 June 2013 amending Directive 2003/98/EC on the re-use of public sector information Text with EEA relevance [2013] OJ L 175/1, rec 21.

71 WP242 (n 14) 18.

72 Ibid 15.

Direct portability is subject to an additional condition – only where it is 'technically feasible' will there be an obligation to comply with a request. Once again, the GDPR falls short, not providing for a definition or explanation.

A basic requirement is that the transmitting and receiving data processing systems be able to communicate, ie be interoperable. However, Recital 68 GDPR solely states that the RtDP 'should not create an obligation for controllers to adopt or maintain processing systems which are technically compatible'. As highlighted by Scudiero, direct portability will extremely 'depend on the availability of standards that make different systems interoperable',[73] which holds true especially considering the RtDP's applicability across sectors.

The likelihood of controllers refusing to comply with portability requests based on technical unfeasibility cannot be underestimated.[74] Although Recital 68 GDPR encourages the development of interoperable formats, there is no legal obligation. In cases where the controller is unwilling to share the individual's personal data with a third party this might seem a good way to circumvent the obligation, undermining the RtDP's purpose.[75]

It is still uncertain in which cases a controller will be able to refuse direct portability based on technical unfeasibility. WP29 understands the 'technical feasibility' concept as (i) a secured communication system between the transferring and receiving controllers, as well as (ii) the capability of the receiving controller's system to receive the incoming data.[76] Nevertheless, it is noteworthy that the GDPR does not oblige the target controller of a portability request to accept the transferred data.[77]

What is technically feasible in practice also depends on the controller's size and sector. What might be technically feasible for big tech giants, might not be for Small and Medium Enterprises (SMEs).[78] It accords with

73 Lucio Scudiero, 'Bringing Your Data Everywhere: A Legal Reading of the Right to Portability' (2017) 3 (1) ECPL 119, 124.

74 Vanberg and Ünver (n 6) 4.

75 Ibid 2.

76 WP242 (n 14) 16.

77 Drexl, 'BEUC Study' (n 43) 109, 147; Kamann and Braun (n 63) 505; Veil (n 46) 603-04; WP242 (n 14) 6.

78 Ruth Janal, 'Data Portability - A Tale of Two Concepts' (2017) 8 (1) JIPITEC 59, 5; Vanberg and Ünver (n 6) 4.

WP29's recommendation to assess technical feasibility on a case-by-case basis.[79]

In any event, even in cases of technical unfeasibility, the data subject still has the right to indirect portability and nothing prevents her from subsequently transferring it to another controller. However, this obviously does not favour reduction of consumers' switching costs.

Furthermore, Drexl argues that the RtDP's exercise should not be limited to *ex-post* situations, ie only after personal data provision.[80] The data subject should be able to request portability also for future data, whereby every new piece of data is automatically sent from the transferring to the receiving controller.[81] This would undoubtfully provide for even stronger control and better reuse of individuals' data, but will ultimately depend on case-law to support it as a right, not merely as a voluntary act of controllers.

3. Conditions for the Right to Data Portability

The RtDP is subject to three cumulative conditions: (i) processing must be based on consent of the data subject or a contract;[82] (ii) the form of processing must be by automated means; and (iii) the object of the processing must be personal data provided by and concerning the data subject.[83]

If any condition is not met, the RtDP cannot be invoked. Thus, each condition will be analysed in the subsections below:

(a) Processing Based on Consent or Contract

Solely processing of personal data based on (i) the data subject's consent, or (ii) a contract between the data subject and the transferring controller, is subject to the RtDP.[84] Data processed on any other legal ground (includ-

---

79 WP242 (n 14) 16.

80 Drexl, 'BEUC Study' (n 43) 110.

81 Some social networks already provide for this possibility. For instance, when posting a photo on Instagram, the user can opt to automatically share it on Facebook, if both accounts are linked.

82 GDPR art 6(1)(a) (general consent), 9(2)(a) (special categories of data), 6(1)(b) (contract).

83 GDPR art 20(1).

84 GDPR art 20(1)(a).

ing legitimate interest under Article 6(1)(f) GDPR), as well as 'processing necessary for performance of a task carried out in the public interest or in the exercise of official authority vested in the controller'[85] are excluded from the RtDP's applicability.

Notwithstanding such limitation, WP29 recommends personal data portability to be adopted as a good practice, even in non-mandatory cases.[86] This will be particularly important for borderline cases, such as employment relations, where the employer generally processes employees' personal data based on legitimate interest,[87] albeit the existence of an employment contract.

Although the idea was to exclude other *lawful* processing grounds, the broad wording also leaves *unlawfully* processed data outside the RtDP's scope.[88] This leads to a situation where the data subject, besides having been subject to an illegal data processing, will not be able to retrieve her data from the controller. In view of this, it is recommended that the RtDP also applies where the individual did not consent.[89]

(b) Processing by Automated Means

The RtDP has a more limited applicability if compared to the GDPR's scope, which also applies for 'processing other than by automated means of personal data which form part of a filing system or are intended to form part of a filing system'.[90] Under Article 20(1)(b) GDPR, the RtDP applies only where the processing is 'carried out by automated means'.

As the GDPR lacks a definition of 'automated means', the only straight forward interpretation is that non-automated means are excluded. Recital 15 provides further guidance, indicating that it does not encompass manual processing, ie processing conducted by an individual. This also seems to be the understanding of WP29, as paper files were deemed excluded.[91]

---

85 GDPR rec 68, art 20(3).

86 WP242 (n 14) 8, fn 16.

87 Helena Ursic, 'Unfolding the New-Born Right to Data Portability: Four Gateways to Data Subject Control' (2018) SCRIPT-ed (forthcoming) <https://ssrn.com/abstract=3176820> accessed 29 June 2018, 16; WP242 (n 14) 8-9.

88 Drexl, 'BEUC Study' (n 43) 152-53; Janal (n 78) 3-4.

89 Ibid.

90 GDPR art 2(1).

91 WP242 (n 14) 9.

Under its ordinary meaning, 'automated' is something operable by machines or computers. Most scholars adopt this path, as the expression is referred to as processing 'by a computer',[92] 'through technology',[93] or using 'data processing systems'.[94] Commonly listed examples include social networks, cloud computing, web services, and smartphone apps.[95] It is also in line with the original proposal, which refers to processing 'by electronic means'.[96]

Furthermore, as the GDPR applies to processing of personal data both wholly or partly by automated means,[97] it remains unclear if this is also the case for the RtDP. One could read the absence of a qualifying adverb (as opposed to the express reference under other provisions[98]), as an indication that the RtDP also applies to partially automated means.[99] Such broader interpretation would be consistent with the RtDP's objective of strengthening individual's control over her data.

However, considering the '*machine-readable format*' requirement,[100] the argument for requiring the process to be conducted wholly by automated means seems more coherent. Should the processing be carried out partially by automated means, the controller would first have to transform the relevant data into a machine-readable format, which represents an additional step and burden.

(c) Personal Data 'Concerning' and 'Provided by' the Data Subject

Article 20(1) GDPR determines that the RtDP is limited to personal data concerning the data subject making the request. This means, *first*, that only

---

92 Lachlan Urquhart, Neelima Sailaja and Derek McAuley, 'Realising the Right to Data Portability for the Domestic Internet of Things' [2017] <https://ssrn.com/abstract=2933448> accessed 28 March 2018, 3.

93 Paul Voigt and Axel von dem Bussche, *The EU General Data Protection Regulation (GDPR): A Practical Guide* (Springer 2017) 383, 10.

94 Ibid 170; Zanfir (n 28) 158.

95 See Swire and Lagos (n 68) 338; Vanber and Ünver (n 6) 2.

96 COM(2012) 11 final (n 54) art 18(1).

97 GDPR art 2(1).

98 For instance, see Article 22(1) GDPR, which refers to a 'decision based *solely* on automated processing'.

99 Lilian Edwards, 'Data Protection: Enter the General Data Protection Regulation' in Edwards L (ed), *Law, Policy and the Internet* (Hart Publishing 2018) (forthcoming) 46.

100 GDPR art 20(1) (emphasis added).

personal data is portable; and, *second*, that the relevant data must identify (currently or potentially) the data subject.

As discussed, the concept of personal data is extremely broad and might encompass a vast array of information. Anonymized data (as long as the anonymization is indeed effective) does not fall within the concept of personal data and, therefore, is outside the RtDP's scope. On the other hand, pseudonymized data is encompassed, as the data subject is identifiable.[101]

Clearly excluded is personal data only concerning other data subjects. Frequently, however, controllers process data relating to multiple data subjects, where the data is intrinsically intertwined, such as in e-mails, telephone and bank records, and group pictures. In such cases, personal data of other data subjects cannot be detached without the data losing its value and purpose. For what value is an e-mail, if one does not know with whom the communication is with? Or a photo with family, friends or colleagues, where other individuals are cut out or blurred?

In line with Recital 68 GDPR,[102] WP29 recommends not taking a too restrictive approach. If the receiving controller's processing does not adversely affect the rights and freedoms of such other data subjects (Article 20(4) GDPR), transmitting controllers should port the data.[103] This would be the case, for example, with a portability request for the content of a webmail or bank account.[104] How exactly this should be assessed by the transmitting controller is unclear and will most likely have to be decided by case-law.

Additionally, the RtDP solely applies to personal data that was provided by the data subject.[105] This restricts the right considerably, as personal data concerning the data subject, but provided to the controller by a third party, is excluded.[106] It even runs against the RtDP's rationale to prevent lock-in effects. For instance, photos and videos depicting the individual,

---

101 GDPR art 11(2) – if the controller cannot identify the data subject, there is no obligation to comply with a portability request. However, the data subject may provide additional information in order to enable the controller to identify her, which might be necessary especially for pseudonymized data.

102 GDPR rec 68, 7th sentence reads as follows: 'where, in a certain set of personal data, more than one data subject is concerned, the right to receive the personal data should be without prejudice to the rights and freedoms of other data subjects in accordance with this Regulation'.

103 WP242 (n 14) 9.

104 Ibid 11.

105 GDPR art 20(1).

106 Veil (n 46) 609.

but posted by another user (even if on the data subject's page/profile) will not be subject to portability. And since social networks are largely about user interaction, not having this data ported might render the RtDP less appealing.

Furthermore, the expression 'provided by' is one of the most contended aspects, which, depending on its interpretation, narrows or broadens the RtDP's scope significantly.[107] The issue lies on the personal data taxonomy based on data origin, which was first discussed in 2014 within the Organisation for Economic Co-operation and Development (OECD).[108]

According to such taxonomy, there are four different categories of personal data: (i) *provided data* – actively and knowingly disclosed by the individual (eg filing of forms and posting on social networks); (ii) *observed data* – observed from the individual and recorded by a third party (eg online cookies and sensors); (iii) *derived data* – new data generated based on other data from the individual (eg computational and notational data); and (iv) *inferred data* – data resulting from probability-based analytic processes (eg statistical and profiling data).[109]

That 'provided data' is within the RtDP's scope has not been questioned, mainly in view of the Commission's emphasis on social networks.[110] On the other hand, passively provided data under the category of observed data has been disputed, as 'providing' is an active act.[111]

A restrictive interpretation would result in the RtDP's inapplicability to data collected through online activity (such as search history, traffic and location data) and connected devices[112] (such as fitness trackers and smart wearables). This would defy the very objective of the RtDP to provide individuals with greater control over their own data in the data economy, and already render the provision outdated at its birth.

---

107 Paul De Hert and others, 'The right to Data Portability in the GDPR: Towards User-Centric Interoperability of Digital Services' [2017] CLSR, 7; Graef, Husovec and Purtova (n 7) 9; Gianclaudio Malgieri, "User-provided personal content' in the EU: digital currency between data protection and intellectual property' (2018) 32 (1) IRLCT 118, 130; Ursic (n 87) 14.

108 OECD, 'Summary of the OECD Privacy Expert Roundtable on 21 March 2014 - Protecting Privacy in a Data-driven Economy Taking Stock of Current Thinking' [2014] DSTI/ICCP/REG(2014)3, 5.

109 Ibid.

110 Drexl, 'BEUC Study' (n 43) 108; Janal (n 78) 3.

111 De Hert and others (n 107) 7; Malgieri (n 107) 130; Veil (n 46) 610.

112 Connected devices can be defined as any device that is connected to other things and persons through mobile communication and which generate data. Drexl, 'BEUC Study' (n 43) 28.

As argued by Drexl and Janal, where personal data is collected from connected devices, data subjects are actually actively and knowingly using the device.[113] Both further reason that the wording of Recital 60 GDPR also speaks in favour of a broader interpretation, as it seems to consider collected data as a way to provide personal data. Similarly, Article 15(g) GDPR also does not clearly distinguish provided and collected data.[114] To reach its full value, WP29 considers that the concept of 'provided by' encompasses both provided and observed data, but not derived and inferred data.[115]

Exclusion of derived and inferred data is perceived as a balancing exercise with the supplier's intellectual effort in creating these forms of data.[116] The restriction prevents competitors from accessing the results of the processing efforts conducted by the first controller or on its behalf. However, it does not enable data subjects to derive the full benefit of their data in the digital economy.[117]

As stated by the Commission, 'like technology, the way our personal data is used and shared in our society is changing all the time' and our 'challenge (...) is to establish a legislative framework that will stand the test of time'.[118] In the data economy, individuals also need portability of their data collected through use of a service or device. Hence, the concept of 'provided by' should be construed as including data actively and knowingly provided, as well as observed data. This, nevertheless, should not prevent the scope's expansion in the future to adapt to new technological challenges.[119]

113 Drexl, 'BEUC Study' (n 43) 108-9; Janal (n 78) 3.
114 De Hert and others (n 107) 7; Malgieri (n 107) 130. Article 15(g) GDPR mentions 'data (...) collected from the data subject'.
115 WP242 (n 14) 10. Also recommended by the EDPS, OJ C 301/1 (n 51) 8, fn 34.
116 Graef, Husovec and Purtova (n 7) 9-10; Voigt and von dem Bussche (n 93) 170-1.
117 Banda (n 28) 45-46; Drexl, 'BEUC Study' (n 43) 156.
118 COM(2010) 609 final (n 17) 18.
119 See Drexl, 'BEUC Study' (n 43) 156, arguing that the exclusion does not protect the interest of making full use of connected devices.

4. The Exception of Rights and Freedoms of Others

The RtDP is not an absolute right, as Article 20(4) GDPR sets forth that it 'shall not adversely affect the rights and freedoms of others'.[120] Which 'others' could be affected by the RtDP is just as little specified as the possible affected rights and freedoms.

The neutral term 'others' renders the provision open to natural and legal persons. It is unclear, however, if such others relate to both the data subject and the controller, or only to the former. Should the reference be to both, then the controller could not raise its own rights and freedoms as impediment to a portability request. In contrast, should it refer solely to the data subject, the possibility would stand.

While WP29 and most literature abide to the first option,[121] this issue will most probably still have to be clarified by case-law. In any event, it is recommendable taking a cautious approach to not provide controllers with an excessively extensive power, undermining the RtDP.[122] Hence, the provision should ideally not allow the controller to raise its own rights and freedoms.

With regard to 'rights and freedoms', when assessing a portability request, controllers must, as discussed, also consider data protection rights of other data subjects in case of multi-personal data. It is coherent with the fact that personal data protection, just as all fundamental rights and freedoms, is not an absolute right. As recognized under Recital 4 GDPR, 'it must be considered in relation to its function in society and be balanced against other fundamental rights, in accordance with the principle of proportionality'.

Nevertheless, considering the broad wording, one may argue that rights of others also cover IPRs. Regarding the right of access, Recital 63 GDPR, determines that it 'should *not adversely affect* the rights or freedoms of oth-

120 Although Article 20(4) refers only to paragraph 1 (indirect portability), the provision was actually intended to also apply to paragraph 2 (direct portability). In the text in preparation for the Trialogue, both rights were within paragraph 2, as paragraph 1 had been omitted. After renumbering, however, the reference was not appropriately amended. Moreover, the final German version of the GDPR still refers to paragraph 2 and, so, German literature refers normally to such paragraph, while commentators form other Member States refer to paragraph 1. See Council Doc ST 15039 2015 INIT (15.12.2015) 110, art 18(2), (2a).

121 Banda (n 28) 49-50; Graef, Husovec and Purtova (n 7) 15; Veil (n 46) 615; WP242 (n 14) 12.

122 Drexl, 'BEUC Study' (n 43) 84-5.

ers, including trade secrets or *intellectual property*' (emphasis added). There is, however, no equivalent provision expressly referring to the RtDP.

Borrowing the wording of Recital 63, WP29 states that

> The *rights* and freedoms *of others* mentioned in Article 20(4) (...) can be understood as "*including* trade secrets or *intellectual property* (...)". Even though these rights should be considered before answering a data portability request, "*the result of those considerations should not be a refusal to provide all information to the data subject*".[123]

There is no explanation on the rationale of such interpretation, but it can be inferred from the RtDP's legislative history, which created a close relationship with the right of access.[124]

It is noteworthy that, notwithstanding such connection, WP29 concludes that it should not result in the controller's refusal to provide all of the individual's data. Consequently, controllers should consider each piece of information separately when assessing a portability request. Refusal to port should only encompass that data adversely affecting an IPR or trade secret of others, not all data.[125]

Finally, the expression 'adversely affect' causes further uncertainty. While some authors characterize it as a balancing clause, which has to be asserted based on the particularities of the case,[126] others understand that the 'RtDP enjoys a lower rank compared to rights and freedoms of others'.[127] According to Drexl, the first construction not only leads to legal uncertainty, but is also not supported by other GDPR language versions.[128]

---

123 WP242 (n 14) 12 (emphasis added).

124 Graef, Husovec and Purtova (n 7) 10.

125 In case of photos in social networks, where the controller can establish that the individual is not the copyright owner, nor has a license, refusal to port should only affect this particular photo, not all personal data.

126 De Hert and others (n 107) 6. Graef, Husovec and Purtova (n 7) 14 also seem to favour a balancing exercise, considering their proposed differentiation based on the subsequent use of ported data.

127 Scudiero (n 73) 126. Note, however, that Scudiero then argues that 'controllers are called to perform a balance', which seems to favour a balancing clause interpretation.

128 Drexl, 'BEUC Study' (n 43) 84, fn 339, indicates the German and French versions, which come closer to full respect of the rights and freedoms of others. As a further example, we can cite the Portuguese version, stating that the RtDP 'não prejudica os direitos e as liberdades de terceiros' (does not prejudice the rights and freedoms of third parties).

In view of this, case-law will certainly be asked to deal with the issue shortly.

Considering the above, there seems to be no reason to exclude IPRs up front from the provision's applicability.

D. Data Portability Beyond Personal Data?

Even though this research's focus lies specifically on the RtDP, it is notable that portability is an emerging and trending concept in the EU, which goes beyond personal data.[129] The Commission already acknowledged data as an essential resource within the data economy and that unjustified restrictions on free flow of data might even jeopardize the full development of the EU data economy.[130] Data portability would be a means to ensure better access to data that, in turn, helps maximizing the value of data for society.[131]

As observed by Drexl, there is no reason to restrict portability to personal data, as lock-in effects also occur in non-personal data scenarios.[132] Most importantly, it is not limited to business-to-consumer (B2C) relationships, but also arises in business-to-business (B2B) settings. The EU legislator seems to understand and support such approach,[133] as two Commission proposals currently under discussion provide for portability related provisions.

The first is under the proposal for a Digital Content Directive, which applies to B2C contracts for supply of digital content, where a price is paid by the consumer or the consumer actively provides a counter-performance other than in money in form of personal or other data.[134] If adopted,[135] it

129 Graef, Husovec and Purtova (n 7) 2; Janal (n 78) 1.

130 COM(2017) 9 final (n 2) 2-3.

131 Commission, 'Commission Staff Working Document on the Free Flow of Data and Emerging Issues of the European Data Economy Accompanying the Document Communication Building a European Data Economy' SWD(2017) 2 final, 47.

132 Josef Drexl, 'Designing Competitive Markets for Industrial Data - Between Propertisation and Access' (2017) 8 (4) JIPITEC 257 para 1, para 157.

133 SWD(2017) 2 final (n 131) 48.

134 COM(2015) 634 final (n 16) art 3(1).

135 The proposal has already been subject to comments and proposed amendments by the Council and the European Parliament. There seems to be a tendency to leave any portability regime for personal data under the scope of the GDPR, but also to end up excluding data portability for non-personal data from the final

will provide consumers with a right to indirect portability after contract termination by the consumer, enabling retrieval of all content provided by her and any other data she produced or generated through the digital content's use.[136]

The second is within the proposal for a Regulation on the Free Flow of Non-Personal Data, which applies to the storage or other processing of electronic non-personal data.[137] Although the Commission's initial idea was to introduce a right to port, it ended opting for a self-regulation for non-personal data.[138] Under the proposed provision, the Commission would encourage and facilitate the development of self-regulatory codes of conduct, to establish best practices on portability.

The above highlights the RtDP's importance, which might be used as a basis to develop other portability schemes in the data economy.[139] Moreover, the relationship between the different portability forms has to be considered under the Commission's proposals to have a coherent outcome.[140]

---

text. For a detailed discussion on the amendments and their potential impact, see Drexl, 'BEUC Study' (n 43) 123-6; Axel Metzger and others, 'Data-Related Aspects of the Digital Content Directive' (2018) 9 (1) JIPITEC 90, 103-5.

136 COM(2015) 634 final (n 16) art 13(2)(c) (for termination in case of non-conformity of the delivered content) and art 16(4)(b) (for termination of long-term contracts).

137 COM(2017) 495 final (n 16) art 2(1).

138 Ibid art 6(1).

139 Josef Drexl and others, 'Position Statement of the Max Planck Institute for Innovation and Competition of 26 April 2017 on the European Commission's "Public Consultation on Building the European Data Economy"' (2017) Max Planck Institute for Innovation & Competition Research Paper No. 17-08 <https://ssrn.com/abstract=2959924> accessed 8 April 2018, para 25.

140 Graef, Husovec and Purtova (n 7) 24; Janal (n 78) 11; Metzger and others (n 135) 103.

III. Personal Data Meets Sui Generis Database Right

As discussed, the RtDP is not an absolute right, since it shall not adversely affect rights and freedoms of others. In view of its broad wording, and considering the RtDP's legislative history and purpose, there are sound reasons to interpret 'rights of others' as encompassing IPRs.

Among the IPR candidates is the SGDR under the DbD. Interesting enough, during discussions of the GDPR's proposal in the Council, the French delegation already raised the potential clash between the RtDP and the SGDR.[141] Hence, the conflict might not have been as silent as suggested.[142]

A. *The EU Database Directive*

Legal protection under the DbD is afforded to databases in any form, while computer programs used in relation thereto are expressly excluded.[143] The DbD's wording is quite broad and technically neutral.[144] Reference to 'any form' comprises all types of databases, regardless of format – electronic and non-electronic databases are covered.[145] The legislator's aim was to provide for 'a wide scope, unencumbered by considerations of a formal, technical or material nature'.[146]

Besides harmonization of national laws in relation to copyright protection of original databases,[147] the DbD also intended to incentivize investment in the production of databases in the EU through the introduction of a new sui generis right – the SGDR.[148] Such right provides database pro-

---

141 Council Doc ST 9897 2012 REV 1 (14.05.2012) 55.

142 Graef, Husovec and Purtova (n 7) 10.

143 DbD art 1(1), (3).

144 DG CONNECT, 'Study in Support of the Evaluation of Directive 96/9/EC on the Legal Protection of Databases – Final Report' (prepared for the Commission by JIIP, Technopolis, and Individual Experts Lionel Bently and Estelle Derclaye) [2018] SMART 2017/0084 (Second Evaluation Report) 4.

145 DbD rec 14.

146 Case C-444/02 *Fixtures Marketing v OPAP* [2004] ECLI:EU:C:2004:697 para 20.

147 DbD rec 2.

148 DbD rec 12.

ducers with an additional layer of protection, resulting in a two-tier protection regime.[149]

The introduction of a novel IPR was justified by the legislator on the significant disparity in the level of investment and legal protection of databases within the EU, but most importantly if compared to the US.[150] It was assumed that the rise of a market for modern information storage and processing systems would require protection against misappropriation to reach its full value.[151]

1. Defining a Database

To be classified as a 'database' under Article 1(2) DbD three cumulative criteria have to be fulfilled: (i) it must consist of a 'collection of independent' elements (ie works, data or other materials); (ii) such elements have to be 'arranged in a systematic or methodical way' and (ii) they must be 'individually accessible'.

The first criterion is that the compilation is a collection of independent elements. There is no minimum number of combined elements to find a database.[152] Although the term 'collection' might resemble a static notion, there is no restriction for the protection of dynamic databases (actually, the protection requirement of 'verification' sustains it, as discussed below).

The fact that the elements have to be independent is of greater relevance.[153] Elements composing audio-visual, cinematographic, literary, or musical works are not considered independent.[154] In the absence of such requirement, there would be a risk of complete overlap with copyright and neighbouring rights.[155] Not only individual pieces of information can con-

---

149 Commission, 'DG Internal Market and Services Working Paper: First Evaluation of Directive 96/9/EC on the Legal Protection of Databases' [2005] <http://ec.europa.eu/internal_market/copyright/docs/databases/evaluation_report_en.pdf> accessed 7 April 2018 (First Evaluation Report) 6.

150 DbD rec 11.

151 DbD recs 12, 39.

152 *Fixtures Marketing* (n 146) para 24.

153 Matthias Leistner, *Der Rechtsschutz von Datenbanken im deutschen und europäischen Recht: eine Untersuchung zur Richtlinie 96/9/EG und zur Umsetzung in das deutsche Urheberrechtsgesetz* (Beck 2000) 372, 46.

154 DbD rec 17.

155 P Bernd Hugenholtz, 'Something Completely Different: Europe's Sui Generis Database Right' in Frankel S and Gervais D (eds), *The Internet and the Emerging*

stitute an independent element, but also a combination of pieces fulfils the requirement.[156]

Furthermore, the CJEU held that independency means an autonomous informative value of the elements, ie when separated from the collection, their contents' value must not be affected.[157] More recently, the Court gave an extensive interpretation thereto by ruling that the value has to be considered from the perspective of the person interested in the separate element.[158] It will be independent if the element is used for financial gain and in an autonomous manner, and provides the person using it with relevant information.

The second criterion is that the elements must be arranged in a systematic or methodical way, but 'it is not necessary for those materials to have been *physically* stored in an organized manner'.[159] It is directly connected to the third criterion of individual accessibility. As long as there is a technical or other means (eg an index, or a particular plan or method of classification) enabling their retrieval from an unorganized collection, the requirements are met.[160]

The result is an overly broad and open-ended definition hardly ever excluding protection.[161] More or less any set of elements can constitute a database under the DbD. For instance, the CJEU has dealt with cases involving databases composed by sports data, legal databases, lists of poems, lists of automobiles, websites selling air travel service and maps.[162]

Importance of New Forms of Intellectual Property (Information Law Series v 37, Kluwer Law International 2016) 205, 211.

156 Case C-490/14 *Verlag Esterbauer* [2015] ECLI:EU:C:2015:735 para 20.

157 *Fixtures Marketing* (n 146) paras 32-3.

158 *Verlag Esterbauer* (n 156) para 37.

159 DbD rec 21 (emphasis added).

160 *Fixtures Marketing* (n 146) para 30.

161 P Bernt Hugenholtz, 'Data Property in the System of Intellectual Property Law: Welcome Guest or Misfit?' in Lohsse S, Schulze R and Staudenmayer D (eds), *Trading Data in the Digital Economy: Legal Concepts and Tools Münster Colloquia on EU Law and the Digital Economy III* (Nomos 2017) 75, 88.

162 Second Evaluation Report (n 144) 5.

2. The Sui Generis Database Right

(a) Protection Requirement

Precondition for protection under the SGDR is the quantitative and/or qualitative substantial investment in either obtaining, verifying or presenting the contents of a database.[163]

(1) The Substantial Investment Requirement

The investment has to be substantial from a quantitative and qualitative perspective. Not only monetary resources deployed by the database maker must be considered, but also human and technical efforts.[164] The quantitative assessment refers to quantifiable resources, such as money and time, and the qualitative assessment to efforts, which cannot be quantified, such as intellectual effort or energy. This means that databases, which do not require high monetary investments, are also protectable, as long as there is a substantial investment of time or effort.

There is no established threshold for the quantum of 'substantial investment' required.[165] Although national courts had different approaches, a relatively low-level of investment sufficed.[166] For instance, the *Bundesgerichtshof* (BGH – German Federal Supreme Court) held that the requirement would be fulfilled if, objectively speaking, no completely insignificant expenses were necessary to create the database.[167]

Even though the absence of a threshold might lead to some uncertainties, a minimum quantum could be discriminatory, excluding small

163 DbD art 7(1).

164 *Fixtures Marketing* (n 146) para 44.

165 Annemarie C Beunen, *Protection for databases: the European Database Directive and its effects in the Netherlands, France and the United Kingdom* (Wolf Legal 2007), 138; Mark J Davison and P Bernt Hugenholtz, 'Football Fixtures, Horseraces and Spin-Offs: the ECJ Domesticates the Database Right' (2005) 27 (3) EIPR 113, 116; Estelle Derclaye, *The legal protection of databases: a comparative analysis* (Edward Elgar 2008) 362, 75; Second Evaluation Report (n 144) 7.

166 Second Evaluation Report (n 144) 7-8.

167 BGH, GRUR 2011, 724 – Case I ZR 196/08 – *Zweite Zahnarztmeinung II* para 23, 'Es reicht aus, wenn bei objektiver Betrachtung keine ganz unbedeutenden, von jedermann leicht zu erbringenden Aufwendungen erforderlich waren, um die Datenbank zu erstellen. Nicht notwendig sind Investitionen von substanziellem Gewicht'.

database makers from protection.[168] The flexible criterion allows for an assessment on an individual basis, including future impact of technological developments.[169]

(2) Investment in Obtaining, Verifying or Presenting

Not any investment counts towards the protection requirement under the SGDR – only substantial investment in (i) obtaining, (ii) verifying or (iii) presenting the contents of a database is relevant. The acts are non-cumulative, which means that either one renders the investment eligible for protection.[170]

The most disputed term was 'obtaining', as it can be construed narrowly or broadly.[171] In *BHB* and *Fixtures Marketing*, the CJEU adopted the former, by distinguishing between creation and collection of the elements.[172] Based on the SGDR's purpose to promote and protect investment, the relevant investment must refer to the creation of the database as such.[173] Consequently, it refers to 'resources used to seek out existing independent materials and collect them in the database, and not to the resources used for the creation as such of independent materials'.[174]

The decision was very welcomed, as it provided a solution (even if partial) for the issue of monopolistic sole-source databases.[175] This was the case in both judgments, where the data composing the databases (list of horseraces and football fixtures, respectively) could not be collected independently, as they were forged by the database makers themselves. As the databases were generated as a by-product of another main activity (ie the organization of horse races and football matches), no substantial investment was actually made on the collection of existing elements, but in their creation. By distinguishing between obtaining and creating, protection for

168 Beunen (n 165) 140; Derclaye (n 165) 91.
169 Beunen (n 165) 141.
170 Ibid 107; Derclaye (n 165) 92.
171 Derclaye (n 165) 92.
172 Case C-203/02 *British Horseracing Board* [2004] ECLI:EU:C:2004:695 (BHB) para 31; *Fixtures Marketing* (n 146) para 40.
173 *BHB* (n 172) para 30.
174 Ibid 31; *Fixtures Marketing* (n 146) para 40.
175 Davison and Hugenholtz (n 165) 114; Derclaye (n 165) 94; Matthias Leistner, 'The Protection of Databases' in Derclaye E (ed) *Research Handbook on the Future of EU Copyright* (Edward Elgar 2009) 427, 437.

sole-source databases was denied, where no substantial investment in obtaining, verification or presentation of the elements created could be evidenced.[176]

Nevertheless, the distinction is not always straightforward.[177] It has been questioned whether data from natural phenomena, stock market rates, or machine-generated data should be categorized as obtaining or creating.[178] Leistner's teleological interpretation provides for some light.[179] Considering that the cases appreciated by the CJEU involved data that were created in the sense of 'made-up' or 'invented', protection would be available only to such pre-existing data that is capable of being independently collected, measured or observed by a third party.

Although the CJEU did not yet decide on a case in this regard,[180] the BGH adopted this approach in the *Autobahnmaut* case.[181] Data collected by a toll company using its tolling system regarding fuel card numbers, vehicle registration numbers, date of the toll journeys and the length of the routes travelled, was considered obtained data.[182] Under BGH's reasoning, such data could be independently collected by a third party, not having been created by the company.

Regarding the act of 'verifying', the CJEU held that it refers to ensuring the reliability of information within the database, as well as monitoring accuracy of the elements collected when of the database's creation or operation.[183] It includes acts of checking, correcting and updating the database's contents,[184] which are of special relevance in case of dynamic databases.[185]

---

176 *BHB* (n 172) para 35.
177 Beunen (n 165) 126; Davison and Hugenholtz (n 165) 115; Hugenholtz, 'Data Property' (n 161) 87; Leistner, 'Protection of Databases' (n 175) 437.
178 Beunen (n 165) 126; Davison and Hugenholtz (n 165) 115; Hugenholtz, 'Data Property' (n 161) 87.
179 Leistner, 'Protection of Databases' (n 175) 438.
180 Matthias Leistner, 'Big Data in the Digital Economy: Legal Concepts and Tools' in Lohsse S, Schulze R and Staudenmayer D (eds), *Trading Data in the Digital Economy: Legal Concepts and Tools Münster Colloquia on EU Law and the Digital Economy III* (Nomos 2017) 27, 28-9, also considers the CJEU's decision in *Verlag Esterbauer* as supporting the distinction.
181 BGH, GRUR 2010, 1004 – Case I ZR 47/08 – *Autobahnmaut*.
182 Ibid para 19.
183 *Fixtures Marketing* (n 146) para 43.
184 Hugenholtz, 'Something Completely Different' (n 155) 212.
185 Beunen (n 165) 134.

Any verification conducted during creation of the elements themselves is ruled out.[186]

Finally, the CJEU found that investment in 'presenting' refers to resources used to give the database its processing information function, 'that is to say those used for the systematic or methodical arrangement of the materials (…) and the organisation of their individual accessibility'.[187] Acts of digitalization of analogue files, creation of a table of contents or thesaurus, or design of user interfaces are within the concept.[188]

(b) Ownership – the Database Maker

According to Article 7(1) DbD, the SGDR is vested in the database maker, ie 'the person who takes the initiative and the risk of investing' (excluding subcontractors).[189] It encompasses natural and legal persons and is consistent with the right's objective to protect investment.[190] This broad definition can lead, however, to significant problems and uncertainties.[191]

Although the DbD does not provide for joint ownership (nor regulates it) the vague criteria to determine the right holder easily leads to such scenario.[192] Whenever two or more persons take the initiative and risk of investment in the creation of a particular database, there will be joint ownership. Especially in cooperative and open innovation networks, as well as in data sharing platforms for connected devices, there is a high probability of co-ownership.[193]

Contractual provisions could regulate it, but it is not uncommon that the parties do not even realize that the resulting database will be jointly owned.[194] Without such awareness, no appropriate provision is included in agreements. Moreover, there might be different bargaining powers, especially in consumer relations.[195] Even if contractually regulated, the outcome might not be the most desired one from a policy perspective.

186 *BHB* (n 172) para 34; *Fixtures Marketing* (n 146) para 50.
187 *Fixtures Marketing* (n 146) para 43.
188 Hugenholtz, 'Something Completely Different' (n 155) 211.
189 DbD rec 41.
190 Leistner, 'Big Data' (n 180) 35.
191 Ibid 35.
192 Second Evaluation Report (n 144) 31.
193 Ibid 31-2; Drexl, 'BEUC Study' (n 43) 77; Leistner, 'Big Data' (n 180) 35.
194 Leistner, 'Big Data' (n 180) 35-6.
195 Ibid.

If the persons creating the database might already have issues in determining who is/are its owner(s), it is even more difficult and burdensome for third parties to precisely know who the database maker is.

(c) Scope of Protection

The SGDR provides an exclusive right to prevent (i) extraction, and (ii) reutilization, 'of the whole or of a substantial part, evaluated qualitatively and/or quantitatively, of the contents of that database'.[196] As a rule, the right lasts for 15 years following the date of completion of the database.[197]

The act of extraction is defined as 'the permanent or temporary transfer of all or a substantial part of the contents of a database to another medium by any means or in any form'.[198] As the SGDR does not confer an exclusive right over information per se,[199] there is no protection against independently created databases where the elements are obtained from other sources than the relevant database.[200] This, however, does not exclude the possibility of an indirect infringement, neither a *de facto* control over the data by the database maker (as discussed below).

No technical reproduction is needed to find an infringing extraction, as the CJEU interpreted the term extensively. It includes 'any unauthorised act of appropriation of the whole or a part of the contents of a database'.[201] It is sufficient that the elements were consulted and copied (even by hand) from the concerned database.[202] Accordingly, good documentation of the creation process is recommended.

The act of reutilisation is specified as 'any form of making available to the public all or a substantial part of the contents of a database, by renting, by on-line or other forms of transmission'.[203] In *BHB*, the CJEU gave the

196 DbD art 7(1).

197 DbD arts 10(1)-(2). In case of substantial change, evaluated qualitatively or quantitatively, to the contents of a database, which results in the database being considered a substantial new investment (also evaluated qualitatively or quantitatively), qualifies the database resulting from that investment for its own term of protection (art 10(3) DbD).

198 DbD art 7(2)(a).

199 Leistner, *Rechtsschutz* (n 153) 146-47.

200 Derclaye (n 165) 107; Leistner, 'Protection of Databases' (n 175) 431.

201 Case C-304/07 *Directmedia Publishing* [2008] ECLI:EU:C:2008:552 para 34.

202 Hugenholtz, 'Something Completely Different' (n 155) 213.

203 DbD art 7(2)(b).

term a broad interpretation, holding that it refers 'to any act of appropriating and making available to the public, without the consent of the maker of the database'.[204]

The provision does not consider the intent or purpose of the acts of extraction or reutilization, providing for an objective infringement test.[205] It is irrelevant, for instance, if the contents of a database are extracted or reutilized to create a competing database or for any other purpose whatsoever.[206]

In the absence of an extraction or reutilization of the database's entire content, the unlawful acts are limited to substantial parts. The intrinsic economic value of the element affected is irrelevant to assess the substantial part.[207] Rather, the substantial investment made by the database maker in obtaining, verifying or presenting the content, as well as the detriment to the data maker's investment should be considered.[208]

In quantitative terms, the substantial part refers to the volume of elements extracted or reutilized from the database in relation to the volume of the database's contents as a whole.[209] The comparison must be with the database subject to extraction or reutilization. For infringement assessment, it is immaterial whether such part subsequently is considered substantial in relation to another database where it is incorporated.[210] The volume threshold has to be established on a case-by-case basis.[211]

A qualitatively substantial part 'refers to the scale of the investment in the obtaining, verification or presentation of the contents of the subject of the act of extraction and/or reutilisation, regardless of whether that subject represents a quantitatively substantial part'.[212] The elements extracted or reutilized have to reflect the money, time and/or effort invested by the database maker. Even a quantitatively small part can represent significant human technical or financial investment.[213] The CJEU thus clearly corre-

204 *BHB* (n 172) para 51.
205 Derclaye (n 165) 119.
206 *BHB* (n 172) para 47.
207 Ibid 72.
208 Ibid 69.
209 Ibid 70.
210 Beunen (n 165) 186; Derclaye (n 165) 110.
211 Derclaye (n 165) 113.
212 *BHB* (n 172) para 71.
213 Ibid 71.

lates the 'substantial investment' requirement for protection and the 'substantial part' requirement for infringement.[214]

In order to prevent the provision's circumvention, Article 7(5) DbD determines that repeated and systematic extraction and/or reutilization of insubstantial parts are unlawful if they (i) conflict with a normal exploitation of the database, or (ii) unreasonably prejudice the legitimate interests of the database maker. The provision intents to avoid extraction of insubstantial parts, which add up and effectively result in the 'reconstitution of the database as a whole or, at the very least, of a substantial part of it'.[215] It is therefore necessary that each insubstantial part differs from each other to jointly make up a substantial part.[216]

In *BHB*, the SGDR's scope was further broadened, as the CJEU ruled that indirect extraction and reutilization are covered.[217] Accordingly, extraction and reutilization based on a third party's copy of the database are equally infringing.[218] The Court's reasoning relies on Article 7(2)(b) DbD, which sets forth that exhaustion after the first sale of a copy only applies to the right to resell that copy.

(d) Exceptions and Limitations

In line with the SGDR's scope, Article 8(1) DbD determines that lawful users might extract and reutilize insubstantial parts of the contents of a database, evaluated qualitatively and/or quantitatively, for any purposes whatsoever. The assessment of an 'insubstantial part' essentially follows the negative of the 'substantial part' test. The provision is binding, whereby any contractual provision to the contrary is deemed null and void.[219] Although not included under the exceptions title of Article 9 DbD, the provision can be considered one.[220]

Article 9 DbD lists exhaustively three optional exceptions, which can be implemented under national legislation: (i) private purposes regarding

---

214 Derclaye (n 165) 111; Davison and Hugenholtz (n 165) 116.
215 *BHB* (n 172) para 87.
216 Leistner, *Rechtsschutz* (n 153) 181.
217 *BHB* (n 172) paras 52-3.
218 Davison and Hugenholtz (n 165) 117.
219 DbD art 15. The CJEU held in *Ryanair* that the lawful user's right is not guaranteed in case of databases not protected under the DbD. Case C-30/14 *Ryanair* [2015] ECLI:EU:C:2015:10.
220 Beunen (n 165) 212.

non-electronic database; (ii) illustration for non-commercial teaching or scientific research; and (iii) public security or an administrative or judicial procedure. While the first two only cover extraction, the latter refers to both extraction and reutilization. Furthermore, the exceptions only cover extraction and/or reutilization of substantial parts (not the whole) of the contents of the database, which are made available to the public by the database maker.

The provision has been very criticized in the literature, as well as in the framework of the evaluations on the DbD.[221] *First*, the DbD does not provide for mandatory exceptions and limitations for the SGDR, which leads to problems in terms of harmonization. *Second*, especially if compared to copyright provisions, the list of exceptions is very limited in scope. In addition, the initially proposed compulsory licensing provision was left out from the DbD's final version.

B. *Intersection between the Right to Data Portability and the Sui Generis Database Right*

After delineating and analysing the RtDP and the SGDR, this chapter now turns to their intersection. Two specific scenarios are discussed; namely, online platforms and connected devices – the first one given the legislator's focus on them when proposing and discussing the RtDP; the second, in view of its growing importance in individual's daily activities.

1. Personal Data as Contents of a Database

As discussed, a database is defined as a collection of independent elements, where they must be systematically or methodically arranged, and individually accessible. The concept of 'independent elements' is quite broad and includes works, data or any other materials. A broad concept also holds true for 'personal data', as any information that may lead to the data subject's identification is covered. Considering that identifiability is highly po-

221 Ibid 212, 228-9; Drexl, 'BEUC Study' (n 43) 81; Annette Kur and others, 'First Evaluation of Directive 96/9/EC on the Legal Protection of Databases - Comment by the Max Planck Institute for Intellectual Property, Competition and Tax Law, Munich' (2006) 37 IIC 551, 556-7; Leistner, 'Big Data' (n 180) 47; First Evaluation Report (n 149) 21-2; Second Evaluation Report (n 144) 15-6.

tentialized by current technologies, a clear distinction between personal and non-personal data seems to be evanescing.

Each piece of personal data is separable from one another and carries an autonomous informative value. Names, addresses, e-mails, location data, and photos are all concomitantly personal data and independent elements that convey a relevant information. In a big data scenario, even the most trivial piece of data might be useful,[222] as well as the combination of two of them.[223] It is, therefore, quite straightforward that personal data is able to form a collection of independent materials.

However, to be classified as a database, personal data still has to be arranged systematically or methodically, and be individually accessible. For instance, telephone directories, lists of e-mail addresses, addresses for mobile phones, names and associated data of persons working at doctor practices, motorway toll databank, and customer lists have already been considered databases under national laws.[224]

The question is, therefore, when personal data provided by the data subject (as per the RtDP) is systematically or methodically arranged, and individually accessible.

(a) Online Platforms

Online platforms contain vast amounts of personal data, which are either active and knowingly provided by the user (such as name, e-mail, age, photos and comments), or collected through observation (such as browsing history, user and purchase preferences, and location data). In view of the identifiability criterion, the majority of the contents created and posted by users will fall under the concept of personal data.[225]

Personal data is usually arranged within online platforms in such a way that it can be individually retrieved. All pieces of information are classified and organized based on certain criteria.[226] Take Facebook, for example, where you have different tabs in the user's profile for each information (timeline, about, friends, photos, etc). Some information is even concomi-

222 Herbert Zech, 'A Legal Framework for a Data Economy in the European Digital Single Market: Rights to Use Data' (2016) 11 (6) JIPLP 460, 467.
223 Drexl, 'BEUC Study' (n 43) 75.
224 Second Evaluation Report (n 144) 5-6, 92, fn 149.
225 Metzger and others (n 135) 103.
226 Graef, *Essential Facility* (n 6) 142.

tantly arranged under multiple categories, such as photos, which are in the timeline, or organized according to its source and date within the 'photo' tab. Electronic retrieval functions are even enhanced through internal search and filter functions.

Consequently, it is possible for online platforms whose content is composed by personal data to be classified as a database under the DbD.[227] Furthermore, each individual user profile/account, as well as the entire online platform can be qualified as a database. In the former case, there is a collection of data on a specific data subject, while in the latter, the collection includes data on several individuals.

(b) Connected Devices

All kinds of daily 'things' are becoming connected to the Internet – from the toothbrush to the coffee machine, going through the front door lock, and entering the car. Although the type of data collected by each connected device is dependent on its function,[228] they for certain increasingly are able to collect personal data through observation, such as location, heartbeats, and temperature.[229]

Data collected by such devices comes from different sources – from integrated sensors, as well as from wireless communication.[230] In addition, their use is usually linked to some service provision or online platform, where individuals provide additional personal data.

All data obtained (as per the DbD) by connected devices, including personal data, will most frequently be structured in databases.[231] The probability of data being collected and not structurally arranged is very remote, as it would render the collection useless.[232] Different pieces of raw data are combined (for example, with additional date, time and location data) to arrange them systematically,[233] and enable its individual retrieval. Conse-

227 Ibid.
228 Drexl, 'BEUC Study' (n 43) 41.
229 As discussed (see II.B), when the Commission referred to home temperature sensors, it recognized that data collected through connected devices might refer to personal and non-personal data. COM(2017) 9 final (n 2) 9.
230 Drexl, 'BEUC Study' (n 43) 41; Second Evaluation Report (n 144) 29.
231 Zech (n 222) 468.
232 Ibid.
233 Drexl, 'BEUC Study' (n 43) 74.

quently, collections of data from connected devices can generally constitute a database under the DbD.[234]

2. Controllers as Database Makers Making a Substantial Investment

For the above databases to qualify for protection under the SGDR, the controller still must qualify as a database maker and there has to be a substantial investment in obtaining, verifying or presenting their contents.

(a) Online Platforms

The operator of an online platform is undoubtedly a controller under the GDPR, as this person, alone or jointly with others, determine the purposes and means of the processing of personal data. There is also little doubt that significant resources are required to set up such platforms to collect personal data from individuals and keep them updated.[235]

The initiative and risk of investment will frequently be taken by the online platform operator. In terms of 'obtaining', the investment in software development does not count, but all effort to make the platform attractive to users and convincing them to use it and provide personal data certainly do.

Under the CJEU's obtaining-creating differentiation, however, a potential issue could arise from content posted by users, which is not pre-existing (such as a photo taken within the social network using the smartphone's camera, filming a live story, or a text spontaneously written by the user).[236] Thus, one could argue that the data is being created, not obtained. However, it is necessary to distinguish between elements created by the database maker itself and by third parties. Taking into consideration the teleological interpretation, it is clear that the data could be independently obtained by third parties, as they are usually not owned or made-up by the

---

234 Ibid 66-7; Hugenholtz, 'Data Property' (n 161) 88; Zech (n 222) 467.

235 Graef, *Essential Facility* (n 6) 481.

236 Graef, *Essential Facility* (n 6) 142-3 also argues that from the obtaining-creating distinction, online platforms could have an issue in claiming Database Right on data that is inferred from the user's use of the platform. However, considering that inferred data is generally not considered data 'provided by the data subject' under the RtDP, it is not of an issue for the specific analysis of this research.

online platform.[237] Another possibility is to consider such live-created contents as composed by two stages – in a first step, the user creates the content (ie takes the photo, films the video or writes the text), on a second, she posts and the database maker obtains it. Therefore, there seems to be no reason to exclude live created contents from the DbD's concept of obtaining.

A substantial investment in verifying the contents is also present, as online platforms constantly gather, check and update user data.[238] Old data is not enough to keep most online platforms attractive, as some data may lose its veracity, such as contact details and preferences.[239] See for instance the messages from Facebook reminding users to update their contact details or to link their account to their mobile numbers, or the e-mails from Instagram and Pinterest showing recent posts and inviting the user to access the platform.

Finally, the effort to make the platform attractive to users is directly tied with the investment in presenting database's contents. The design of a user-friendly interface is key for online platforms, which leads to constant investment for improvements.

Considering the above, it is possible for online platforms to rely on the SGDR whenever there is evidence of a substantial investment in obtaining, verifying and presenting the data.[240]

(b) Connected Devices

The controller in case of a connected device might be its manufacturer and/or any third-party providing services there through, depending on who decides how and why personal data is processed. With regard to the database maker, the situation is far from clear.

There is currently no unanimity whether databases originating from connected devices are protectable under the SGDR.[241] While Drexl and Leistner understand that the SGDR's low threshold may easily lead to pro-

---

237 Some of the major online platforms and social networks (such as Facebook, Instagram, Snapchat, TripAdvisor, Twitter and YouTube) recognise under their Terms of Use/Service the user's ownership and/or copyright on the content she posts.

238 Graef, *Essential Facility* (n 6) 488.

239 Ibid 504.

240 Ibid 143.

241 Second Evaluation Report (n 144) 30.

tection,[242] the Second Evaluation Report on the DbD concludes that it likely does not, as the databases' generation is closely related to data creation.[243]

From the Report's statement, the main issue for recognizing the SGDR is the obtaining-creating rule.[244] However, as discussed, data collected through observation by connected devices could fall within 'obtaining' under the teleological interpretation. The data is not made-up by the database maker and could (at least in theory) be independently obtained by others. This also seems to be the BGH's approach in *Autobahnmaut*.[245]

Although investment in developing connected devices or software does not amount towards the obtaining requirement,[246] setting up infrastructure for measuring, obtaining or documenting might.[247] The constant collection and updating of the database's contents fulfils the verification requirement. In addition, structuring the data methodically or systematically also counts for the presentation requirement.[248] Therefore, databases from connected devices might also frequently rely on the SGDR.[249]

The question in whom the SGDR will be vested is less clear. It could be argued that the individual acquiring or using the device also makes an investment and takes the risk to have her data collected.[250] However, considering the 'initiative' requirement, it will usually be vested in the connected device's manufacturer.[251] Consequently, the manufacturer might concomitantly be the controller and the database maker.

3. The Sui Generis Database Right as 'Rights of Others'

As discussed, there are no sound reasons to interpret 'rights of others' under the RtDP as excluding IPRs. Notwithstanding its sui generis character

242 Drexl, 'BEUC Study' (n 43) 68; Leistner, 'Big Data' (n 180) 27-8.
243 Second Evaluation Report (n 144) Executive Summary, ii.
244 Drexl, 'BEUC Study' (n 43) 70.
245 *Autobahnmaut* (n 181).
246 Ibid 63.
247 Leistner, 'Big Data' (n 180) 29, 37.
248 Ibid 29.
249 Drexl, 'BEUC Study' (n 43) 85; Same understanding of the majority of experts consulted for the Second Evaluation Report (n 144) 131.
250 Second Evaluation Report (n 144) 32.
251 Drexl, 'BEUC Study' (n 43) 77; Leistner, 'Big Data' (n 180) 37; Second Evaluation Report (n 144) 32.

and the peculiarities surrounding its protection requirements, the SGDR can be considered a type of IPR.[252] Thus, it could be invoked by controllers to refuse a portability request.[253]

Although the preferred approach is that 'others' does not include the controller, considering the unclear wording, one cannot disregard the risk of courts interpreting the provision otherwise. Moreover, even in cases where the recommended interpretation is adopted, the SGDR could still be claimed in the event of joint ownership, which might be more common than expected.

4. Data Portability Request as Extraction or Reutilization of the Contents of a Database

The remaining question is if a portability request can adversely affect the database maker's SGDR. A potentially adverse effect on the SGDR could arise from an unlawful act affecting the right's investment protection function, ie one that is not permitted under its scope, nor excused by an exception.

The Commission, when referring to the absence of a RtDP in 2012, stated that 'there is also no explicit right for the individual to *extract* his/her own personal data (...) from an application or service'.[254] This indicates that the RtDP possibly comes very close to the database maker's right to prevent extraction of the contents of its database.

In view of *BHB*'s ruling that the SGDR's scope covers indirect extraction or reutilization, both the data subject, as well as the receiving controller might commit an infringing act. The likelihood of the latter would be higher where the receiving controller offered the data subject some kind of incentive to exercise her RtDP.[255] The experience with the telecom number portability showed that suppliers might very well be willing to give discounts, extra credits or the alike to convince someone to port.

As the individual's personal data composes the database's contents, the exercise of the right to both direct and indirect portability will result in a permanent transfer of the personal data content to another medium. Whether the extraction amounts to a substantial or insubstantial part, will

252 Beunen (n 165) 14.

253 Drexl, 'BEUC Study' (n 43) 83-4.

254 SEC(2012) 72 final (n 20) 28 (emphasis added).

255 Graef, Husovec and Purtova (n 7) 16.

essentially depend on the definition of the database from where content is retrieved.

In view of this, a database maker could attempt to influence the assessment's outcome by narrowing the database's size.[256] Rather than considering the entire universe of online platform or connected devices users, the database maker could limit the database to the contents relating to the specific individual requesting portability. While in the first case, the volume extracted could be considered insubstantial in comparison to the whole, in the second it would likely be substantial. Consequently, a portability request could potentially be understood as an unlawful extraction.

The database maker's right to prevent the reutilization of substantial parts of its database's contents might also be infringed. The data subject or the receiving controller could make the content available to the public by online transmission, for example.[257] Whenever the concerned personal data is made available to an indeterminate number of persons (such as on an online platform), a 'making available to the public' could be found and, thus, an infringing act.

Even in case of an extraction or reutilization of insubstantial parts there might still be an infringement if the acts are repeated and systematic. A possible interpretation would consist of reiterated portability requests from one data subject to the same controller.[258] However, it seems unlikely that such reiterated requests from one individual would include insubstantial parts if compared to a database concerning her, or that the substantial parts would amount to a substantial part in relation to the whole database.

A possible extensive interpretation would consist of portability requests from different data subjects to the same controller, whereby such individuals received an incentive from a third party to make the request. In this case, the sum of the personal data contents of different individuals could represent a substantial part of the whole database and an indirect act of extraction by the receiving controller.

256 Beunen (n 165) 189-90.

257 Graef, Husovec and Purtova (n 7) 15.

258 Although reiterated portability requests are not prohibited under the GDPR, Article 12(5) GDPR determines that excessive portability requests, in particular because of their repetitive character, allow the controller to charge a reasonable fee or even refuse the request. The GDPR does not determine what would be considered 'repetitive', or in which cases the controller would actually be able to refuse the portability instead of only charging a fee.

The above acts could still not infringe if one of the exceptions from the SGDR comes into play,[259] but none seems applicable to the RtDP. The only potential candidate is the extraction for personal use in case of an indirect portability, where the data subject, after receiving her personal data from the original controller, decides not to forward it to a new controller, but keep it for herself on a private device. However, this hypothesis is very limited and does not meet the RtDP's rationale.

The above analysis shows that there is indeed a possible clash between the RtDP and the SGDR, whereby the second could be invoked to bar the first.[260]

259 As the exceptions are not mandatory, applicability would further depend whether and to what extend they were implemented under national laws.

260 Drexl, 'BEUC Study' (n 43) 83-4.

IV. Do We Need a Re-Designed Approach for the Data Economy?

A. *Potential Issues Arising from the Intersection*

The intersection between the RtDP and the SGDR does not remain without consequences. Considering that it is recognized that the RtDP also has a competition and consumer law dimension, this Chapter first analyses the issues arising within these areas. Subsequently, taking especial account of the First and Second Evaluation Reports in the DbD, it discusses whether the SGDR is still fit for the data economy.

1. Competition Law Impacts

(a) Lock-In Effects

The rationale behind the RtDP was precisely to reduce consumer lock-in, by enabling individuals to take their personal data and switch providers more easily. Competition and innovation in the data economy were expected to be concomitantly promoted,[261] as portability reduces entry barriers for personal data dependent business models.[262]

Although the RtDP seems to tackle all issues at once, it remains to be seen how it will work in practice. *First*, because it essentially depends on data subjects actively invoking the RtDP.[263] This is directly tied to user awareness and the limited extend of the right's scope. *Second*, there are other reasons, besides lock-in, why individuals might not want to change, such as network effects.[264] Nonetheless, both could be influenced by market players' willingness to provide additional portability incentives. This might likely happen considering the experience in the telecom sector and

---

261 WP242 (n 14) 5.
262 Graef, *Essential Facility* (n 6) 154-5.
263 Graef, Husovec and Purtova (n 7) 19; Vanberg and Ünver (n 6) 6.
264 Network effects are characterized by a service/product's value increasing with the increase of the number of its users. Social networks and search engines are typical examples. Graef, *Essential Facility* (n 6) 44ff.

the expected increase of undertakings seeking to acquire data to provide new products and/or services, or set new business models.[265]

However, lock-in effects are aggravated if database makers are able to rely on their right to prevent portability of personal data contents. In certain circumstances, there is already a *de facto* control over the individual's personal data,[266] while the SGDR grants an additional layer of exclusivity.[267] The database maker is the only one in possession of the personal data, being able to control access, whilst the individual has no alternative other than remaining with the supplier to use her data.

Connected devices are particularly problematic in this regard,[268] especially in relation to historic data. Take for instance an energy smart meter – the individual might also be interested in her 'old' consumption data, as it can be used by a third party to provide a comparison with other suppliers and allow the user to switch. Even though third parties could have collected, in theory, the data independently when the manufacturer did it, this is usually not the case. And the data cannot be collected anymore as the relevant point in time has passed. Consequently, only the database maker is in possession of the relevant personal data and might want to prevent third parties from accessing it by claiming its SGDR.[269]

While the RtDP might not be the magic pill envisioned by the Commission, the possibility of the SGDR barring the right's exercise undeniably does not leave data subjects, nor competition in the data economy in a better position.

(b) Big Data Scenarios

Big data analysis, characterized by a high volume, velocity and variety of data,[270] has an enormous potential in terms of better solutions and decision-making.[271] It increasingly relies on data collected by connected de-

265 COM(2017) 9 final (n 2) 13.
266 Leistner, 'Big Data' (n 180) 37.
267 Drexl, 'BEUC Study' (n 43) 85.
268 Ibid 70.
269 Ibid 19.
270 Drexl, 'Designing Competitive Markets' (n 132) para 26; Graef, *Essential Facility* (n 6) 131.
271 Drexl, 'Designing Competitive Markets' (n 132) para 19.

vices,[272] combining large datasets from diverse sources, to reach different results.

Data's non-rival nature allows personal data collected and processed for one initial purpose to be reused for a second one, without preventing the first.[273] As individuals become increasingly depended on their personal data to switch or enjoy different or new value-added products/services, they have a legitimate interest in unlocking it.[274] The RtDP now precisely enables individuals to retrieve their personal data from one controller and share it with others, permitting different big data analytics in favour of the individual.

Besides the possibility of changing to a service provider that renders better data analytics, individuals might also have an interest in combining their different personal datasets for new analysis. Take for instance historic data on body functions and data location: separately they might not indicate a health condition, but when analysed together they potentially can lead to a diagnosis.

Access to data is therefore essential for big data.[275] The SGDR, in contrast, generally represents a legal barrier for data access and reuse in big data settings, as the insubstantial parts exception is insufficient.[276] If the whole contents or a substantial part is extracted, the SGDR is infringed. Big data requires the largest possible (ideally complete) datasets from various sources to derive (reliable) outputs. Precisely because of this, data subjects have a legitimate interest in accessing all of their personal data for a reliable analysis.

Therefore, if the database maker can prevent personal data portability based on its SGDR, possible positive effects that could be derived from the RtDP will be undermined, to the detriment of individuals' legitimate interest.

---

272 Second Evaluation Report (n 144) 1.
273 Drexl, 'Designing Competitive Markets' (n 132) para 67.
274 Drexl, 'BEUC Study' (n 43) 157.
275 Second Evaluation Report (n 144) 40.
276 Leistner, 'Big Data' (n 180) 32, 48.

(c) Data Portability Refusal as Abuse of Dominance

In view of the RtDP's competition law dimension, portability refusal may lead to liability under Article 102 TFEU[277] for abuse of dominance.[278] Although there has been no competition law case so far dealing with access to personal data, as the underlying ground here would be the controller's SGDR, recourse can be taken from cases on refusal to license IPRs.[279]

Two prerequisites must be met for Article 102 TFEU to apply: (i) the controller has to enjoy a market dominance, and (ii) such dominant position must be abused by the controller. Besides the difficulty of establishing the relevant market and dominance in data markets,[280] it already demonstrates the limited applicability to portability. While individuals can exercise their RtDP vis-a-vis any controller, regardless of its size,[281] competition authorities can enforce the provision only against dominant undertakings.[282]

Moreover, the circumstances of the case have to amount to an abuse. Only in exceptional circumstances, a refusal to license constitutes abuse of dominance, whereby four cumulative conditions have to be met – the refusal must (i) relate to an indispensable product/service; (ii) exclude competition in the downstream market; (iii) prevent the emergence of a new product to consumers' prejudice;[283] and (iv) not be objectively justified.[284] Applicability of such rule is quite challenging.

To what extend data, and in particular personal data, can fulfil the indispensability requirement is doubtful.[285] As only 'technical, legal or even economic obstacles capable of making it impossible or even unreasonably difficult'[286] amount to indispensability, most data do not meet the thresh-

277 Treaty on the Functioning of the European Union [2012] OJ C 326/47 (TFEU).

278 Graef, Husovec and Purtova (n 7) 21; Graef, Verschakelen and Valcke (n 6) 7; Vanberg and Ünver (n 6) 6.

279 Drexl, 'Designing Competitive Markets' (n 132) para 123.

280 Drexl, 'BEUC Study' (n 43) 36-7.

281 This has been criticised in the literature, as the RtDP would be too burdensome for SMEs and could represent a disincentive to innovate. Graef, Verschakelen and Valcke (n 6) 9; Swire and Lagos (n 68) 351-65.

282 Graef, Verschakelen and Valcke (n 6) 8; Vanber and Ünver (n 6) 14.

283 Drexl, 'BEUC Study' (n 43) 77, fn 288 notes that this new product rule provides for a higher standard of abuse in case of refusal to license if compared to refusal to deal.

284 Case T-201/04 *Microsoft* [2007] ECLI:EU:T:2007:289 paras 331-2.

285 Van der Auwermeulen (n 6) 62.

286 Case C-7/97 *Bronner* [1998] ECLI:EU:C:1998:569 para 44.

old, since they are generally available and can be independently collected.[287] In limited circumstances, it could be argued that personal data is an indispensable input, as in case of historic data[288] or business models characterised by strong network effects.[289]

The exclusion from competition limits the provision to undertakings,[290] ie data subjects cannot rely on it, where no subsequent transfer to another controller takes place after an indirect portability. Moreover, taken jointly with the new product rule requirement, it prevents application where the new controller wishes to provide a competing product/service in the principal market. As the RtDP's rationale is to reduce lock-in, it is expected that direct portability requests will be made for competing providers.

In sum, although portability refusal based on the controller's SGDR can potentially amount to a competition law infringement, it definitively would not cover all cases. While enforcement by competition law authorities cannot be entirely excluded, only in very limited cases it would provide for a remedy. It is thus necessary to look outside the realm of competition law to find a suitable solution.

2. Consumer Protection Law

In the data economy, the traditional distinction between consumer and data protection law becomes blurred. With the increasing use of personal data in exchange for services or integrated with IoT, 'many data protection issues also become consumer issues, and vice versa'.[291] Processing of personal data affects individuals both as data subjects and consumers,[292] which is the reason why 'data protection also has to be considered as a key element and an integral part of modern consumer protection law'.[293]

Promoting the interests of consumers and ensuring a high level of consumer protection is dictated by Article 169 TFEU. Consumer empower-

287 Drexl, 'Designing Competitive Markets' (n 132) para 135.

288 Banda (n 28) 23.

289 Drexl, 'Designing Competitive Markets' (n 132) para 135.

290 Drexl, 'BEUC Study' (n 43) 36-7.

291 Natali Helberger, Frederik Zuiderveen Borgesius and Agustin Reyna, 'The Perfect Match? A Closer Look at the Relationship Between EU Consumer Law and Data Protection Law' (2017) 54 (5) CML Rev 1427, 1428.

292 Ibid 1459.

293 Drexl, 'BEUC Study' (n 43) 54.

ment[294] is intrinsically aligned with the RtDP's purpose to provide individuals with greater control.[295] By allowing data subjects to retrieve and share their personal data with other controllers, the RtDP strengthens the individual's position as consumer, redressing the imbalance in commercial transactions with suppliers.[296] It unlocks the reuse of personal data, from which individuals are increasingly depended to access 'better' or alternative services.

Contrarily, portability refusal could seriously weaken consumers' position. Considering that consumer law also seeks to protect individuals as weaker parts in commercial transaction,[297] it could potentially be applied to enforce portability.[298] Different from competition law, it could reach all types of controllers, as no dominance or abusive behaviour must be demonstrated.[299] Nevertheless, as the refusal here would be based on the controller's SGDR, it is quite unclear if and to what extend current consumer protection rules could take prevalence over an IPR.

3. Suitability of the Sui Generis Database Right for the Data Economy?

Whether the DbD is still fit-for-purpose in the data economy has been recently addressed in the Commission's second evaluation.[300] The study finds that it is an outdated legal framework, which does not cope with technological changes anymore,[301] as database creation 'has evolved (...) from the manual gathering of existing data, over automatic processes of data collection, even to automatic creation of data'.[302]

As in the first evaluation,[303] there is no evidence that the SGDR was able to fulfil its purpose to stimulate investment in database creation, nor influence EU's database competitiveness.[304] Database makers' decision to invest

---

294 Helberger, Zuiderveen Borgesius and Reyna (n 291) 1436.

295 This also explains why the RtDP can be considered more a provision of consumer protection. Drexl, 'Designing Competitive Markets' (n 132) para 155.

296 De Hert and others (n 107) 3.

297 Helberger, Zuiderveen Borgesius and Reyna (n 291) 1436.

298 Graef, 'Blurring Boundaries' (n 60) 4; Graef, Husovec and Purtova (n 7) 24.

299 Graef, 'Blurring Boundaries' (n 60) 4.

300 Second Evaluation Report (n 144).

301 Ibid Executive Summary, iv.

302 Ibid 26.

303 First Evaluation Report (n 149) 5.

304 Second Evaluation Report (n 144) Executive Summary, iv.

in database production seems to disregard the SGDR,[305] which supports the inquiry whether a legal-economic incentive is indeed necessary.

The SGDR has been subject to substantial critique in this regard.[306] IPRs are an exception to the general rule of free competition, where the underlying idea is to provide incentive to innovate in exchange for a long-term gain in static efficiency. However, they also affect third parties' ability to innovate, resulting in dynamic inefficiencies. In sum, the goal is to provide the ideal level of incentive, which in case of the SGDR apparently completely failed.

As sole-source databases demonstrate, database production is frequently a by-product of other main business activities. It would have been created regardless of the SGDR's incentive, considering that the database maker's aim is not the database production (as it is the case of online platforms and connected devices). Practice shows that the SGDR is opportunistically used *ex-post*.[307] This also means that the database maker is able to recoup its investment from other sources,[308] running against an incentive problem to justify protection under the SGDR.[309]

Moreover, the study indicates that databases are usually further protected by other means besides the SGDR, such as contractual terms and technological measures.[310] This supports the conclusion that the SGDR strengthens the *de facto* control that some database makers already have over the database's contents. Not unsurprisingly, the SGDR is reported as a 'strong right, coming very close to protecting data as such'.[311]

Therefore, the question whether the SGDR is suitable for the data economy essentially depends if one understands that there is need for more exclusivity or access to data.[312] Considering the harmful effects of data monopolies and the growing necessity of data in daily interactions, the latter

305 Ibid.

306 Ibid 40.

307 Ibid 95.

308 See for instance the *Autobahnmaut* case (n 181), where the toll company was already receiving compensation by the German government for the service provision, or the payment of a price for a connected device – Drexl, 'BEUC Study' (n 43) 74.

309 This is one of the main arguments underlying the so-called 'spin-off doctrine'. See Davison and Hugenholtz (n 165) 114.

310 Second Evaluation Report (n 144) Executive Summary, ii.

311 Ibid 59.

312 Drexl, 'BEUC Study' (n 43) 69.

seems most appropriate.[313] The SGDR's expansion to a data ownership alike right[314] lacks legal and economic grounds.[315]

As discussed, the SGDR' broad protection can lead to a sole-source database issue even where data is obtained and not created,[316] such as with historic data. With access to data being compromised, there might be a foreclosure of secondary markets, which are data dependent, creating anticompetitive entry barriers.[317] The SGDR's inefficient and outdated dispositions to foster innovation were highlighted by some study participants, who considered it as 'an obstacle to key activities in the market, such as [data] sharing, re-use and mining'.[318] This is perfectly exemplified by its conflict with the RtDP, which potentially prevents reuse of personal data.

In view of this, the answer to the question whether the SGDR is still suitable for the data economy has to be answered in the negative. The right does not seem appropriate to fulfil its goals, may be regarded as excessively generous by affording protection even where not needed, and might have significant anticompetitive effects.

B. Possible Ways Forward

The fact that the SGDR is able to bar the RtDP creates a barrier for the free flow of personal data, which contradicts the assumption that unjustified restrictions on such free flow might hamper the data economy.[319] Considering the above-identified issues, as well as the RtDP's pro-competitive character, there seem to be valid grounds to conclude that the SGDR needs to undergo a change to be fit for the data economy.

Even though the SGDR is apparently not (yet) regularly invoked,[320] its potential (harmful) role within the data economy should not be underesti-

---

313 Ibid; Hugenholtz, 'Data Property' (n 161) 98-9; Leistner, 'Big Data' (n 180) 43, 55-6.

314 The Commission is discussing the possibility of introducing a data ownership alike right (the data producer's right). COM(2017) 9 final (n 2); SWD(2017) 2 final (n 131).

315 Drexl and others (n 139) para 8.

316 Second Evaluation Report (n 144) 39.

317 Ibid 46.

318 Ibid 27.

319 COM(2017) 9 final (n 2) 2-3.

320 Drexl, 'BEUC Study' (n 43) 85; Leistner, 'Big Data' (n 180) 55.

mated, nor ignored.[321] Thus, possible ways forward to address its clash with the RtDP are discussed below with the aim of ensuring the RtDP's effectiveness.

1. Case-Law Interpretation

Leaving the conflict's resolution to case-law is a logic option, as the judicial system is the one tasked with interpreting the law when it is vague, unclear or silent. National courts apply EU law on a daily basis, which, however, might lead to inconsistencies across Member States. Through a preliminary ruling referral, the CJEU has jurisdiction to issue a binding decision on a matter of interpretation and validity of EU law.[322]

In view of this, the timeframe can be somewhat problematic. It could take a few years until the CJEU issues a ruling on the interface between the RtDP and the SGDR, which would keep the uncertainty and possibly inconsistency across the EU for some while, potentially preventing the free flow of personal data. Until such decision is issues, significant harm could also be done to the EU's data economy development.

Nevertheless, predicting the outcome of the CJEU's decision is probably the major challenge.[323] In addition to Article 20(4) GDPR referring to 'rights and freedoms of others', Article 13 and Recital 48 DbD explicitly set forth that the DbD's provisions shall be without prejudice to data protection legislation. The absence of a clear hierarchy of norms certainly does not render the question any simpler.

As discussed, the expression 'adversely affect' is also far from clear. The reason why some authors consider it as a balancing clause might lie on the data protection's status as fundamental right. The right to personal data protection is recognized under Article 16 TFEU and regarded as a fundamental right under Article 8 Charter,[324] as well as a human right under Article 8 ECHR, as part of the right to respect for private and family life.[325]

Data subjects' right of access is even expressly recognizes under Article 8(2) Charter. Considering that the RtDP might be regarded as a logical

321 Drexl, 'BEUC Study' (n 43) 85.

322 TFEU art 267.

323 Drexl, 'BEUC Study' (n 43) 85.

324 Charter of Fundamental Rights of the European Union [2012] OJ C 326/391 (Charter).

325 Convention for the Protection of Human Rights and Fundamental Freedoms (European Convention on Human Rights, as amended) (ECHR).

derivative thereof, its fundamental right status could be understood as extending to the RtDP.

Should the RtDP be recognized as a fundamental right, it would necessarily have to be balanced with other fundamental rights, such as IPRs under Article 17 Charter. Although it might be unclear whether Article 17(2) would also be read as including sui generis rights, such as the SGDR, it cannot be excluded upfront. The balancing exercise would have to take account of the principle of proportionality, but its outcome would still be uncertain.

On the other hand, as the RtDP's purpose is not to enhance the data subject's moral interests, it can also be understood as being more of a consumer protection rule,[326] falling outside the realm of data protection. Should the RtDP not be regarded as a fundamental right, the CJEU could possibly held that the 'rights and freedoms of others' (including the SGDR) always take precedence over the RtDP. Such outcome could significantly endanger the effectiveness of the RtDP, as discussed

Even in case of a decision favouring the RtDP, the risk of it being reversed in the future cannot be disregarded. The legal uncertainty that this possibility causes was precisely one of the justifications why the Second Evaluation Report cogitates including a compulsory licensing for the SGDR.[327]

2. Repeal of the Database Directive or the Sui Generis Database Right

Repealing the DbD as a whole, or even merely the SGDR, would certainly solve the issue of the SGDR being raised by controllers as a bar to the RtDP.[328] These radical possibilities have actually been considered in both DbD's evaluations by the Commission,[329] in view of the DbD's hardly discernible impacts.

On the other hand, it must be noted that the DbD provided at least for some benefit in the internal market, such as some greater legal certainty and harmonization,[330] and that the SGDR seems to work in certain con-

326 Drexl, 'Designing Competitive Markets' (n 132) para 155.

327 Second Evaluation Report (n 144) 39.

328 It would have an immediate effect for new databases, but probably a medium to long term effect for databases already protected by the SGDR before repeal, as acquired rights would have to be respected.

329 First Evaluation Report (n 149) 25-6; Second Evaluation Report (n 144) 126.

330 Second Evaluation Report (n 144) Executive Summary, ii.

texts.[331] Both Evaluation Reports also confirm that once legislation is put in place, undoing it is very challenging.[332] Hence, a complete withdrawal is probably unrealistic and eventually unnecessary.[333]

Although abolishment is a way forward, it is not proportionate for the specific purpose of ensuring the RtDP. Moreover, to ponder such drastic option, an in-depth analysis of other issues and impacts would be required to determine its suitability, which goes far beyond this research's scope.

3. Amendment of the Database Directive

The possibility of amending the DbD has been considered by both Evaluation Reports[334] and, therefore, could constitute a concrete way to solve the conflict.

Considering that in numerous situations no need for incentive to invest in database production was identified, an option could be to reduce the SGDR's scope to exclude by-product databases. Thus, the SGDR would be limited to cases where protection is really needed to recoup investment. Although such option could substantially reduce cases of spin-off databases (such as online platforms and connected devices) and, consequently, of conflicts with the RtDP, it would still leave room for some problems. *First*, any amendment to the SGDR's scope would be risky, as its untested wording would be subject to courts' scrutiny,[335] leading to uncertainty (likewise the case-law interpretation). *Second*, depending on the amendment, it might be insufficient for both the RtDP, as well as other portability schemes or general data access issues.

A more radical alternative in line with the above would be transforming the SGDR in a registrable IPR.[336] Protection would also be afforded only in those situations where an incentive is necessary, as database makers would have to actively seek it.[337] Besides a possible increase in administrative costs, a registrable SGDR could lead to a rise in strategic registra-

331 Leistner, 'Protection of Databases' (n 175) 454-5.
332 First Evaluation Report (n 149) 5, 25; Second Evaluation Report (n 144) 126.
333 Kur and others (n 221) 552; Leistner, 'Protection of Databases' (n 175) 450-1.
334 First Evaluation Report (n 149) 26; Second Evaluation Report (n 144) Executive Summary, vi.
335 First Evaluation Report (n 149) 26.
336 Leistner, 'Big Data' (n 180) 38; Second Evaluation Report (n 144) 139.
337 Leistner, 'Big Data' (n 180) 38; Second Evaluation Report (n 144) 71.

tion.[338] Once controllers realize that protection could assist them in preventing sharing of users' personal data with third parties based on the RtDP, there could be a flood of applications from online platforms operators and connected device manufactures.[339]

In view of the issues with monopolistic databases, the idea of introducing a compulsory licensing system has been revisited.[340] It could also be used to prevent the SGDR from barring the RtDP, as the database maker would be obliged to grant a license upon the data subject's and/or the new controller's request, whereby the parties would have to agree upon a price.

The Second Evaluation Report lists three main reasons to consider a compulsory license: (i) doubts whether case-law can prevent sole-source databases; (ii) importance of access to data in the context of big data and connected devices; and (iii) the risk of CJEU's obtaining-creating rule being reversed.[341] On the other hand, it also notes some downsides, mainly related to the system's precise delineation, ie its scope, remuneration and administrative matters.[342] There is currently also no EU-wide compulsory licensing scheme for any IPR. In the absence of a unitary SGDR, national laws would ultimately regulate and implement it, which could lead to harmonization problems.[343]

Leistner defends that, where the SGDR holds valuable under the incentive to invest ratio, the compulsory license would have to be subject to a Fair, Reasonable and Non-Discriminatory (FRAND) payment.[344] Besides the difficulty in negotiating and setting such fees, in certain situations there seems to be no solid reason for remuneration. The database maker was (and might even continue to be) able to recoup its investment from other sources, such as from the price paid by the data subject for the service and/or the connected device,[345] or advertising revenue in online platforms.

Although a theoretical option, a compulsory license would probably fall short for the SGDR-RtDP clash. If, for instance, the system would be sub-

338 Ibid.

339 This could be minimized with a joint reduction of the SGDR's scope, but then again, similar problems could arise.

340 Derclaye (n 165) 280; Leistner, 'Big Data' (n 180) 43; Second Evaluation Report (n 144) 41.

341 Second Evaluation Report (n 144) 39.

342 Ibid 41.

343 Ibid 42.

344 Leistner, 'Big Data' (n 180) 43-5.

345 Drexl, 'BEUC Study' (n 43) 83.

ject to competition law rules,[346] similar problems on the applicability of Article 102 TFEU would be encountered. Moreover, it could result in a further layer of data access regulation, possibly incentivizing *de facto* holders to claim the SGDR.[347]

A statutory licensing system, through the introduction of an exception to the SGDR subject to remuneration, could be another option. Different from the compulsory licensing system, no prior authorization from the right owner is needed and, generally, the law sets the fee *ex-ante*.[348] By removing the price negotiation element, it is less burdensome for the party interested in the IPR.

This comes very close to Graef, Husovec and Purtova's proposal of a purpose-specific exception to IPRs with a claim for fair remuneration.[349] The authors distinguish between two scenarios: (i) use of the personal data by the own data subject (ie indirect potability without subsequent transfer to a new controller), and (ii) use by a new controller.[350] In the first, considering the data subject's legitimate interest to use her own personal data, the RtDP would prevail free of charge. In the second, however, where the new controller would usually have to seek a license, remuneration would be owed to the original controller.[351]

From a practical standpoint, the distinction is somewhat problematic.[352] *First*, in case of indirect portability, it would be tough to control a subsequent transfer to one or more new controllers. There could even be a significant gap between receipt from the original controller and the transfer. *Second*, identifying the database maker might not be an easy task, especially in case of joint ownership. *Third*, in view of data's non-rival nature, it could be hard to prove that the data was extracted from the database of a particular controller – the exact same data could theoretically have been provided to multiple controllers.

In addition, similar to the compulsory licensing, this option would 'transform a right to exclude to a less intrusive right to be paid',[353] enabling the database maker to recoup its investment. Nonetheless, as dis-

346 Leistner, 'Big Data' (n 180) 44; Second Evaluation Report (n 144) 42.
347 Ibid 76.
348 Derclaye (n 165) 282.
349 Graef, Husovec and Purtova (n 7) 15-8.
350 Ibid 14.
351 Ibid 17-8.
352 Ibid 18, the authors also recognize that the concept would lead to several complications, including administrative costs.
353 Ibid.

cussed, there are cases where such a remuneration might have no ground to be in place. Considering that the new controller is under no obligation to receive ported personal data, this could also reduce such controller's incentive to accept it, to the detriment of data subjects.

Adding the RtDP to the list of exceptions to the SGDR could be a further possibility. Different from the statutory and compulsory licensing systems, no remuneration would be mandated. Its applicability could be general or purpose-specific (for example, considering the subsequent use's purpose, as discussed). In case of general applicability, it could undermine, in theory, the incentive necessary of the creation of certain databases. Also, if too narrowly designed (ie mentioning specifically the RtDP), the exception would not take account of other types of portability which might be enacted in the future, possibly not standing the test of time.

Furthermore, the options of compulsory license, statutory license and exception to the SGDR have also a common drawback – they could incentivize database makers to not claim the SGDR to avoid being subject to the provision. Considering that the database maker will usually be the one best qualified to evidence that its investment fulfils the requirements, applicability of the DbD could probably be circumvented without great efforts.[354] Where such database makers are *de facto* controllers of the databases' contents, they could try to prevent applicability of RtDP based on a different right or freedom (such as trade secrets protection[355] or right to conduct business[356]), retaining the uncertainty.

4. Preferred Approach

Balancing the above options, the one repealing the DbD as a whole or only the SGDR are clearly the first to be disregarded. It is disproportionate for purpose of ensuring portability of personal data and does not account for

354 This would be further supported by CJEU's decision in *Ryanair* (n 219), holding that the DbD does not apply to databases which do not fulfil the conditions for protection.

355 For instance, Facebook already denied access to a user's full personal data based on the Irish Data Protection Acts, which 'carves out an exception to subject access requests where the disclosures in response would *adversely affect trade secrets or intellectual property*'. E-mail from Facebook to Max Schrems (28 September 2011) <http://www.europe-v-facebook.org/FB_E-Mails_28_9_11.pdf> accessed 1 September 2018 (emphasis added).

356 Graef, Husovec and Purtova (n 7) 12, fn 66.

other potential issues and consequences. This leaves essentially two realistic possibilities: case-law interpretation or amendment of the DbD.

While case-law interpretation might appear as an obvious candidate, the outcome's unpredictability is very risky for the data economy's development. The CJEU has already given the SGDR a quite broad and generous interpretation. Should the Court rule that Article 20(4) GDPR requires full prevalence of the SGDR over the RtDP, this would not only harm individuals with regard to access to their personal data, but also represent a negative precedent for other cases of legitimate interest in accessing non-personal data.

Both the case-law interpretation and the discussed amendment options also have a common disadvantage: as the SGDR is frequently an additional layer of protection, database makers could easily circumvent any judgments or provisions favouring the RtDP over the SGDR by simply not invoking the right. Their investment decision is usually not based on the existence of protection, nor is the recoupment of such investment dependent thereupon. This urges for a coordinated approach, which takes the big picture of the data economy into consideration.

Rather than focusing solely on the RtDP, the better solution would consist in the inclusion of a broader non-waivable exception in the DbD, whereby regimes on data access rights prevail over the SGDR.[357] The Max Planck Institute for Innovation and Competition has proposed such a non-waivable data access right (not restricted to personal data) for those with a legitimate interest in such access,[358] under which the RtDP can be regarded as a specific category. The Second Evaluation Report even considered such access right proposal and concluded that it could be enshrined under an amended version of DbD,[359] which is coherent with the identified need to guarantee greater access to data.

Although providing for an exception within the DbD would already solve the conflict of the RtDP with the SGDR, it would not suffice in a broader context, as it could be circumvented. To be effective, the access right would also have to take account of other laws (such as privacy, trade secrets and contract law) to provide for a consistent and systematic

357 Drexl, 'BEUC Study' (n 43) 83, 85, 161.

358 Drexl and others (n 139) para 20. For further comments and analysis on the particularities of such proposed data access right regime, see Drexl, 'BEUC Study' (n 43) (more specifically on connected devices) and Drexl, 'Designing Competitive Markets' (n 132).

359 Second Evaluation Report (n 144) 115.

regime.[360] This would require analysis and empirical studies in different sectors to identify where exactly amendments are necessary, which also speaks against a case-law option, which cannot provide for such a far-reaching and coordinated possibility.

Besides already covering the RtDP, the general access right exception has some clear advantages. *First*, it could encompass possible future forms of data portability (beyond personal data), as well as other general access regimes developed based on the needs of new data business models. This broader provision would render it more time resistance. *Second*, database makers 'law shopping' could be at least reduced, as it avoids circumventing one access provision within a legislation by choosing to invoke another right. *Third*, any particularities on possible FRAND remuneration could be discussed outside the DbD system,[361] enabling different solutions for the particularities of each case.

Unfortunately, however, the Commission (supported by the Second Evaluation Report) has decided to not conduct a legislative intervention at the DbD for now.[362]

---

360 Ibid 42.

361 Drexl, 'BEUC Study' (n 43) 83.

362 Ibid 141; COM(2018) 232 final (n 3) 9.

V. Conclusion

This research aimed to explore and redefine the interface between the RtDP and the SGDR, taking particular account of the data economy's context. The intersection identified between the two rights was not as silent as suggested, and leaves open a significant loophole, which can undermine the RtDP's effectiveness to the prejudice of data subjects' legitimate interests and the development of EU's data economy.

A broad interpretation of the RtDP to include observed data under its scope is favoured, as it would otherwise render the provision outdated at its birth. This construction allows data subject to retrieve their personal data not only from online platforms, but also from connected devices. The SGDR's far-reaching definition and low threshold, on the other hand, hardly excludes protection, leading to a real potential clash within those scenarios of personal data provided by individuals.

Opportunism in the SGDR's enforcement against the RtDP is not implausible and might even strengthen the database maker's monopolistic position in case of sole-source databases. In view of the RtDP's pro-competitive dimension and the legitimate interest of individuals to access their data, as well as the fact that the SGDR does not seem fit for the data economy, this research argued for alternatives to ensure the RtDP's effectiveness.

Although repealing the DbD as a whole or only the SGDR would clearly solve the clash with the RtDP, these radical options are not proportionate for the specific purpose of ensuring the RtDP. Nevertheless, such possibilities should not be discarded upfront – an in-depth analysis of other issues and impacts should be conducted to determine its suitability, which, however, goes far beyond this research's scope.

Case-law interpretation is a logic option, but the unpredictability of a judgment's outcomes is extremely risky. Leaving the issue for courts that might not be acquainted with a wide-ranging picture of the data economy can produce undesirable results, foreclosing data-driven markets. Furthermore, the possibility of database makers circumventing a decision favouring the RtDP over the SGDR cannot be disregarded.

Going through a coordinated approach by introducing an exception in the DbD mandating prevalence of data access rights regimes over the SGDR seems particularly favourable for the data economy, because besides already encompassing the RtDP, it could include possible future forms of data portability (beyond personal data), as well other general access regimes. This gives the provision the required flexibility to stand the test of time, as well as the possibility for the EU to consider a broader action though the recognition of a non-waivable data access right (not restricted to personal data) for those with a legitimate interest in such access.

Therefore, this research calls the Commission to reconsider its initial decision to not take immediate legislative action to reform the DbD. The intersection between data protection and IPRs might not be very intuitive in a first moment, as exemplified by the absence of any analysis of the SG-DR's impacts on the RtDP within the framework of the Second Evaluation Report. However, such encounters tend to increase significantly within the data-driven economy and neglecting the potential harmful effects that they might cause, could endanger the EU data economy's development significantly.

List of Works Cited

Monographies and Articles

Banda C, *Enforcing Data Portability in the Context of EU Competition Law and the GDPR* (Master Thesis, MIPLC 2017) 61

Beunen AC, *Protection for databases: the European Database Directive and its effects in the Netherlands, France and the United Kingdom* (Wolf Legal 2007) 436

Davison M and Hugenholtz PB, 'Football fixtures, Horseraces and Spin-Offs: The ECJ Domesticates the Database Right' [2005] 27 (3) EIPR 113

De Hert P and others, 'The right to Data Portability in the GDPR: Towards User-Centric Interoperability of Digital Services' [2017] CLSR

Derclaye E, *The legal protection of databases: a comparative analysis* (Edward Elgar 2008) 362

Drexl J, 'Designing Competitive Markets for Industrial Data – Between Propertisation and Access' (2017) 8 (4) JIPITEC 257 para 1

—— and others, 'Position Statement of the Max Planck Institute for Innovation and Competition of 26 April 2017 on the European Commission's "Public Consultation on Building the European Data Economy"' (2017) Max Planck Institute for Innovation & Competition Research Paper No. 17-08 <https://ssrn.com/abstract=2959924> accessed 8 April 2018

——, 'Data Access and Control in the Era of Connected Devices – Study on Behalf of the European Consumer Organization BEUC' (2018) BEUC <https://www.beuc.eu/publications/beuc-x-2018-121_data_access_and_control_in_the_area_of_connected_devices.pdf> accessed 9 June 2019

Edwards L, 'Data Protection: Enter the General Data Protection Regulation' in Edwards L (ed), *Law, Policy and the Internet* (Hart Publishing 2018) (forthcoming)

Engels B, 'Data Portability Among Online Platforms' (2016) 5 (2) IPR

Graef I, *Data as Essential Facility: Competition and Innovation on Online Platforms* (Doctoral Thesis, KU Leuven Faculty of Law 2016) <https://lirias.kuleuven.be/bitstream/123456789/539854/1/Final+draft+PhD+-+Inge+Graef+-+Data+as+Essential+Facility+-+30+May+2016.pdf> accessed 15 March 2018

——, 'Blurring Boundaries of Consumer Welfare: How to Create Synergies between Competition, Consumer and Data Protection Law in Digital Markets' (2016) <https://ssrn.com/abstract=2881969> accessed 15 March 2018

——, Husovec M and Purtova N, 'Data Portability and Data Control: Lessons for an Emerging Concept in EU Law' (2017) DP 2017-041 Tilburg Law School Legal Studies Research Paper Series No. 22/2017 <https://ssrn.com/abstract=3071875> accessed 26 March 2018

——, Verschakelen J and Valcke P, 'Putting the Right to Data Portability into a Competition Law Perspective' (2013) <https://ssrn.com/abstract=2416537> accessed 28 March 2018

Helberger N, Zuiderveen Borgesius F and Reyna A, 'The Perfect Match? A Closer Look at the Relationship Between EU Consumer Law and Data Protection Law' (2017) 54 (5) CML Rev 1427

Hugenholtz PB, 'Something Completely Different: Europe's Sui Generis Database Right' in Frankel S and Gervais D (eds), *The Internet and the Emerging Importance of New Forms of Intellectual Property* (Information Law Series v 37, Kluwer Law International 2016) 205

——, 'Data Property in the System of Intellectual Property Law: Welcome Guest or Misfit?' in Lohsse S, Schulze R and Staudenmayer D (eds), *Trading Data in the Digital Economy: Legal Concepts and Tools Münster Colloquia on EU Law and the Digital Economy III* (Nomos 2017) 75

Janal R, 'Data Portability - A Tale of Two Concepts' (2017) 8 (1) JIPITEC 59

Kamann HG and Braun M, 'Art. 20 Recht auf Datenübertragbarkeit' in Ehmann E and Selmayr M (eds) *Datenschutz-Grundverordnung: DS-GVO* (2nd edn, Beck 2018) 495

Kur A and others, 'First Evaluation of Directive 96/9/EC on the Legal Protection of Databases - Comment by the Max Planck Institute for Intellectual Property, Competition and Tax Law, Munich' (2006) 37 IIC 551

Leistner M, *Der Rechtsschutz von Datenbanken im deutschen und europäischen Recht: eine Untersuchung zur Richtlinie 96/9/EG und zur Umsetzung in das deutsche Urheberrechtsgesetz* (Beck 2000) 372

——, 'The Protection of Databases' in Derclaye E (ed) *Research Handbook on the Future of EU Copyright* (Edward Elgar 2009) 427

——, 'Big Data in the Digital Economy: Legal Concepts and Tools' in Lohsse S, Schulze R and Staudenmayer D (eds), *Trading Data in the Digital Economy: Legal Concepts and Tools Münster Colloquia on EU Law and the Digital Economy III* (Nomos 2017) 27

Malgieri G, ''User-provided personal content' in the EU: digital currency between data protection and intellectual property' (2018) 32 (1) IRLCT 118

Metzger A and others, 'Data-Related Aspects of the Digital Content Directive' (2018) 9 (1) JIPITEC 90

Purtova N, 'The Law of Everything. Broad Concept of Personal Data and Future of EU Data Protection Law' (2018) 10 (1) LIT 40

Scudiero L, 'Bringing Your Data Everywhere: A Legal Reading of the Right to Portability' (2017) 3 (1) EDPL 119

Swire P and Lagos Y, 'Why the Right to Data Portability Likely Reduces Consumer Welfare: Antitrust and Privacy Critique' (2013) 72 MdLRev 335

Urquhart L, Sailaja N and McAuley D, 'Realising the Right to Data Portability for the Domestic Internet of Things' (2017) <https://ssrn.com/abstract=2933448> accessed 28 March 2018

Ursic H, 'Unfolding the New-Born Right to Data Portability: Four Gateways to Data Subject Control' (2018) SCRIPT-ed (forthcoming) <https://ssrn.com/abstract=3176820> accessed 29 June 2018

Van der Auwermeulen B, 'How to Attribute the Right to Data Portability in Europe: A Comparative Analysis of Legislations' (2017) 33 (1) CLSR 57

Vanberg AD and Ünver MB, 'The Right to Data Portability in the GDPR and EU Competition Law: Odd Couple or Dynamic Duo?' (2017) 8 (1) EJLT

Veil W, 'Artikel 20 – Recht auf Datenübertragbarkeit' in Gierschmann S and others *Kommentar Datenschutzgrundverordnung* (Bundesanzeiger 2018) 590

Voigt P and von dem Bussche A, *The EU General Data Protection Regulation (GDPR): A Practical Guide* (Springer 2017)

Zanfir G, 'The right to Data Portability in the Context of the EU Data Protection Reform' (2012) 2 IDPL 149

Zech H, 'A Legal Framework for a Data Economy in the European Digital Single Market: Rights to Use Data' (2016) 11 (6) JIPLP 460

International Treaties

Convention for the Protection of Human Rights and Fundamental Freedoms (European Convention on Human Rights, as amended) (ECHR)

EU Legislation

Charter of Fundamental Rights of the European Union [2012] OJ C 326/391

Directive 95/46/EC of the European Parliament and of the Council of 24 October 1995 on the protection of individuals with regard to the processing of personal data and on the free movement of such data [1995] OJ L 281/31 (Data Protection Directive – DPD)

Directive 96/9/EC of the European Parliament and of the Council of 11 March 1996 on the legal protection of databases [1996] OJ L 77/20 (Database Directive – DbD)

Directive 2000/31/EC of the European Parliament and of the Council of 8 June 2000 on certain legal aspects of information society services, in particular electronic commerce, in the Internal Market ('Directive on electronic commerce') [2000] OJ L 178/1

Directive 2013/37/EU of the European Parliament and of the Council of 26 June 2013 amending Directive 2003/98/EC on the re-use of public sector information Text with EEA relevance [2013] OJ L 175/1

Regulation (EC) No 45/2001 of the European Parliament and of the Council of 18 December 2000 on the protection of individuals with regard to the processing of personal data by the Community institutions and bodies and on the free movement of such data [2001] OJ L 8/1

Regulation (EU) 2016/679 of the European Parliament and of the Council of 27 April 2016 on the protection of natural persons with regard to the processing of personal data and on the free movement of such data, and repealing Directive 95/46/EC [2016] OJ 2 119/1 (General Data Protection Regulation – GDPR)

Treaty on the Functioning of the European Union [2012] OJ C 326/47 (TFEU)

EU Cases

Case C-7/97 *Bronner* [1998] ECLI:EU:C:1998:569

Case C-203/02 *British Horseracing Board* [2004] ECLI:EU:C:2004:695 (BHB)

Case C-444/02 *Fixtures Marketing v OPAP* [2004] ECLI:EU:C:2004:697

Case T-201/04 *Microsoft* [2007] ECLI:EU:T:2007:289

Case C-304/07 *Directmedia Publishing* [2008] ECLI:EU:C:2008:552

Case C-70/10 *Scarlet Extended* [2011] ECLI:EU:C:2011:771

Case C-131/12 *Google Spain* [2014] ECLI:EU:C:2014:317

Case C-30/14 *Ryanair* [2015] ECLI:EU:C:2015:10

Case C-490/14 *Verlag Esterbauer* [2015] ECLI:EU:C:2015:735

Case C-582/14 *Breyer* [2016] ECLI:EU:C:2016:779

Case C-434/16 *Nowak* [2017] ECLI:EU:C:2017:994

German Cases

BGH, GRUR 2010, 1004 – Case I ZR 47/08 – *Autobahnmaut*

BGH, GRUR 2011, 724 – Case I ZR 196/08 – *Zweite Zahnarztmeinung II*

Publications and Communications from Authorities

Article 29 Data Protection Working Party, 'Guidelines on the Right to Data Portability' [2017] 16/EN WP242 rev 01 (WP29 Guidelines)

Commission, 'DG Internal Market and Services Working Paper: First Evaluation of Directive 96/9/EC on the Legal Protection of Databases' [2005] <http://ec.europa.eu/internal_market/copyright/docs/databases/evaluation_report_en.pdf> accessed 7 April 2018 (First Evaluation Report)

——, 'A comprehensive Approach on Personal Data Protection in the European Union' (Communication) COM(2010) 609 final

——, 'Proposal for a Regulation of the European Parliament and Of the Council on the protection of individuals with regard to the processing of personal data and on the free movement of such data (General Data Protection Regulation)' COM(2012) 11 final

——, 'Impact Assessment Accompanying the General Data Protection Regulation and the Directive on the Protection of Individuals with Regard to the Processing of Personal Data by Competent Authorities for the Purposes of Prevention, Investigation, Detection or Prosecution of Criminal Offences or the Execution of Criminal Penalties, and the Free Movement of such Data' (Commission Staff Working Paper) SEC(2012) 72 final

——, 'A Digital Single Market Strategy for Europe' (Communication) COM(2015) 192 final

——, 'Proposal for a Directive of the European Parliament and of the Council on Certain Aspects Concerning Contracts for the Supply of Digital Content' COM(2015) 634 final

——, 'Building a European Data Economy" (Communication) COM(2017) 9 final

——, 'Commission Staff Working Document on the Free Flow of Data and Emerging Issues of the European Data Economy Accompanying the Document 'Building a European Data Economy' (Communication)' SWD(2017) 2 final

——, 'Proposal for a Regulation of the European Parliament and of the Council on a Framework for the Free Flow of Non-Personal Data in the European Union' COM(2017) 495 final

——, 'Towards a Common European Data Space' (Communication) COM(2018) 232 final

——, 'Summary Report of the Public Consultation on the Evaluation of Directive 96/9/EC on the Legal Protection of Databases' (Consultation Results, 6 October 2017) <https://ec.europa.eu/digital-single-market/en/news/summary-report-public-consultation-legal-protection-databases> accessed 7 March 2018

Council Doc ST 9897 2012 REV 1 (14.05.2012)

Council Doc ST 10614 2014 INIT (06.06.2014)

Council Doc ST 15039 2015 INIT (15.12.2015)

DG CONNECT, 'Study in Support of the Evaluation of Directive 96/9/EC on the Legal Protection of Databases – Final Report' (prepared for the Commission by JIIP, Technopolis, and Individual Experts Lionel Bently and Estelle Derclaye) [2018] SMART 2017/0084 (Second Evaluation Report)

EDPB, 'Endorsement of GDPR WP29 guidelines by the EDPB' [2018] Endorsement 1/2018

EDPS, 'EDPS Recommendations on the EU's Options for Data Protection Reform' [2015] OJ C 301/1

European Parliament, 'Report on the Proposal for a Regulation of the European Parliament and of the Council on the Protection of Individuals with Regard to the Processing of Personal Data and on the Free Movement of such Data (General Data Protection Regulation)' A7-0402/2013

IDC, 'European Data Market – Final Report' [2017] SMART 2013/0063

OECD, 'Summary of the OECD Privacy Expert Roundtable on 21 March 2014 - Protecting Privacy in a Data-driven Economy Taking Stock of Current Thinking' [2014] DSTI/ICCP/REG(2014)3

Others

E-mail from Facebook to Max Schrems (28 September 2011) <http://www.europe-v-facebook.org/FB_E-Mails_28_9_11.pdf> accessed 1 September 2018